The Uncaged Mind

How to Break Free from Your Subconscious
Conditioning to Live a Wildly Fulfilling Life

Katie Potratz

Published by Four Eagles Publishing,

Newcastle, Australia

Tel: (+61) 417 785 921;

www.foureaglespublishing.com

First published in Australia in 2023

Copyright © 2023 Katie Potratz

All rights reserved.

No part of this book may be reproduced in any form or by any electronic or mechanical means, including information storage and retrieval systems, without written permission from the author, except for the use of brief quotations in a book review. Requests to the publisher should be directed to *support@foureaglespublishing.com*

The information in this book is the author's opinion only. Readers should not rely on the general information given in this book as a substitute for professional advice. The author and publisher cannot accept responsibility for any losses, damages or adverse effects that may result from the use of information contained in this book.

A catalogue record for this book is available from the National Library of Australia

ISBN: 978-0-6454618-7-9

ISBN: 978-0-6454618-8-6 (ebook)

For my daughter, Nataleigh, and my son, Jon.

I love you more than you will ever know.

May you always know how limitless you are.

CONTENTS

INTRODUCTION: The Strength of Belief   01

PART 1:
THE ILLUSIONS

CHAPTER 1: Bound by Limitation   07
CHAPTER 2: The Deception of Duality   19
CHAPTER 3: Internally Unsafe   31
CHAPTER 4: Separation Breeds Suffering   43

PART 2:
THE HEALING

CHAPTER 5: Crossing the Threshold   57
CHAPTER 6: Accepting the Rejected   71
CHAPTER 7: Bringing Light to the Darkest Parts   83
CHAPTER 8: Solving the Chronic Equation   93

PART 3:
THE GROWTH

CHAPTER 9: Shedding the Skin   109
CHAPTER 10: Beyond the Self   119
CHAPTER 11: Spiraling Upward   131
CHAPTER 12: Take Flight   137

ACKNOWLEDGEMENTS   140
ABOUT THE AUTHOR   142

"All problems are illusions of the mind."

ECKHART TOLLE

INTRODUCTION:

The Strength of Belief

I'm going to tell you something that might make you uncomfortable but if you're honest with yourself, I think you'll agree.

You've been brainwashed.

The brainwashing I'm talking about was self-inflicted. Indeed, we've all been brainwashing ourselves our entire lives, and we're *really good at it*. I would argue that our minds are the best brainwashing systems there are. It's impossible to not get sucked into the illusions our minds feed us. Why? Because it starts right from birth.

These illusions are so compelling that no matter what kind of evidence we have that contradicts those lies, we *just keep believing them*. An entire lifetime can easily be spent lost in those illusions; most are. Much of mine was.

The consequences of those illusions are what we commonly refer to as the mental health crisis – crippling anxiety, life-threatening depression, debilitating insecurity, and generational trauma. Many people aren't aware that they can also lead to many chronic physical conditions as well. I'm talking everything from autoimmune diseases to mystery aches and pains.

These illusions have a very real and tangible effect on our lives because we *believe them*. The strength of that belief causes a ripple effect that impacts our thoughts, behaviors, emotional reactions, and even our physical body.

They are so intricately woven into every part of our lives that they impact our sense of self, our relationships and all of our decisions. Although they are seemingly impenetrable, those illusions *can* be broken. And when they break, a lot of what we thought was real comes crumbling down with them.

We call this *healing*.

I used to think healing was all rainbows, butterflies, and marshmallow clouds, but I've learned a thing or two since then. Healing is shattering the illusions that were causing your suffering, and it's rarely pretty. In fact, it can be downright confronting.

But that's not why we do it. We do it for what's on the other side. *That's where the rainbows are.*

We do it for the freedom, the sense of peace, and the weightlessness that can be felt in every cell of our body. We do it to end our suffering.

The only reason I'm even here right now writing this book is because of a crack. I watched an illusion crack and begin to crumble, and that experience was the catalyst that changed the trajectory of my life. It was in the cracking that I began to realize I'd brainwashed myself into believing so many things that weren't true. I started to grasp the enormity of those lies and the suffering they had caused me. That single crack gave me an opportunity to believe something new.

Since then, I've made it my mission to help as many people as possible break the illusions that are causing their suffering. The deeper I dove into my own healing the more I understood that our subconscious minds are running the show. I became a Certified Clinical Hypnotherapist and have spent hundreds of hours working with individuals on their deepest subconscious blocks – from anxiety and depression to shame and self-doubt and even chronic pain and disease. This experience has given me an intimate view of the inner workings of our minds. It's shown me just how powerful those illusions are and how life-changing it is to break them.

In the following chapters I will walk you through the most influential illusions we humans experience, giving you real life examples of how they show up and how they are shattered. In Part One I will break down the four biggest illusions that are causing lifelong suffering. I'll demonstrate how these illusions are causing a wide range of symptoms such as anxiety, shame, persistent negative thoughts, self-doubt, chronic pain, disease and more. I'll be sharing not only how these illusions have shown up in my own life and how they've limited me, but also in many of the individuals I've served over the years.

In Part Two, I pull back the curtain to show you what really happens when we heal, detailing what it takes to break free from those illusions. Come along as I share real life stories of individuals who've healed everything from anxiety and self-sabotage to chronic pain and disease.

Finally, Part Three walks you through the growth that occurs as those illusions come crashing down. Discover what becomes possible when you remove the imaginary limitations of the mind.

Imagine having a front row seat in discovering what your mind is truly capable of. Imagine removing the invisible barriers that have been keeping you stuck in endless cycles of fear, doubt, and shame.

If you're open to it, this book can offer a single crack; one that can shake the very foundations of those illusions and give you an opportunity to shatter what's been holding you back.

Are you ready to see what your mind is truly capable of?

PART 1
THE ILLUSIONS

"You are a victim of the rules you live by."

JENNY HOLZER

CHAPTER 1:

Bound by Limitation

An unassuming summer day in 2015. My husband, two-month-old daughter and I were on a road trip, camped in some RV park off the highway. It was a misty morning in August, and I was sitting alone in the passenger's seat after having escaped to read in the quiet while my daughter napped.

The book I was reading was unlike any book I had read before. It was one you might find in the Self-Help section of the bookstore, although I wouldn't know because I didn't buy it. In fact, when this book was given to me I had absolutely no interest in reading it at all.

It sat on my bookshelf for weeks until something compelled me to pick it up and take it on that trip. So there I was sitting in the quiet, while everything I thought I knew came crashing down.

I was dumbfounded.

I paused and glanced up. It wasn't what was written on the page, but rather the light bulb that just went on in my head. It's as if the world suddenly seemed bigger – but at the same time, everything felt closer, as if it was now within reach.

It was the moment that my familiar illusion – the only thing I'd ever known – just *cracked*. For the first time I was seeing through it, like peering up at the night sky and seeing the limitless universe that stretches beyond the blanket of clouds.

That moment changed everything.

In the following weeks and months, I felt like I was living in a parallel universe. Nothing had actually changed, and yet everything felt different. I started to do things I had only ever dreamed of doing. I started seeing things that I had previously overlooked. My perception of myself was morphing right before my eyes.

Back then I didn't really understand what was happening. I didn't know what exactly had changed, but I knew it was big.

It's been nearly eight years since that day. Within those eight years I've come to learn a lot about the mind. I've had the rare opportunity to get an inside look at the intricacy of the mind and how it operates. It's given me the understanding that everything about life is completely subjective. You are not experiencing life as it is, but rather *as you are*.

> *Right from birth we begin to weave the tapestry of our unique reality. Every experience we encounter provides us with neutral information with which we create meaning. Unknowingly we are creating subconscious associations to everything in life, some negative, some positive, and those associations are the basis of our beliefs and conditioning.*

Our early years are easily the most impactful years of our lives. We are taking in neutral information from the people we interact with, the situations we find ourselves in, and the environment around us and creating meaning based on how it makes us feel. As children, our minds are completely open, like sponges we are absorbing everything around us. In the first decade of life, we will come to conclusions about ourselves that will ultimately impact who we become and the life we create.

Your parents or caregivers are your biggest role models. You will unconsciously look to them to understand love, your value, your role in relationships, the meaning of life, and everything else. What we don't understand as children is that our parents are just people. They carry their own limitations and trauma that they will knowingly or unknowingly imprint onto their children. How each individual child perceives that information will determine the meaning they assign to it. That's why siblings who were raised by the same parents in the same household can grow up with massively different models of the world. They may go on to create very different lives because when they were weaving their reality, they perceived the same situations differently.

There's an old story of twin boys raised by an alcoholic father. One boy grew up and became an alcoholic. When asked what happened to create this fate he replied, "I watched my father." The other boy grew up and never touched a drop of alcohol. When asked why, he replied, "I watched my father." Our unique perception of life is what creates reality. Our parents and our upbringing do not determine our future, it simply gives us neutral information that we use to create meaning.

In those early years your reality is influenced by every interaction and experience you go through. The people you spend time with, the experiences you have, the way things make you feel will all leave a lasting imprint. When information is presented to you at that young age you don't have the capacity to subjectively analyze it, you just absorb it. Children's minds are incredibly malleable because they collect and store information and experiences in their subconscious mind. Young children haven't yet developed their critical mind, which means they take everything at face value. For example, if a situation has made a child feel unworthy or ashamed, then their understanding may be that it's them who is unworthy or shameful, and that understanding becomes a belief and is stored in their subconscious, having the potential to create lasting effects on their self-perception.

So much of who you are and what you believe began in those early years of childhood. As your mind is developing, your experiences will shape what you perceive as normal, acceptable, and expected.

Your reality is like a bubble created around your life based on all of the neutral information you've gathered. Within the bubble is everything that is real to you; everything that feels accessible and realistic. Outside of the bubble exists everything that feels "unreal". That which lies outside of your bubble is not actually *un-real*, and often we recognize that others can have it, but for ourselves, it feels out of reach.

Of course, this realm of reality isn't something that we can see or touch, but rather it's something that we unknowingly believe. It's an invisible boundary to what is achievable and realistic in our life. This realm of reality creates the Illusion of Limitation. It creates the false sense that some things are unrealistic or impossible.

The Illusion of Limitation is what holds people back from their deepest desires. The belief that it's not possible for them will keep that dream just out of reach. I experienced this in my own life and even though I could see that others could have, do and be what I wanted, I still didn't believe it was possible for me. The Illusion of Limitation would keep me from even taking the first step.

> *The meaning we've assigned to neutral information can cause us to believe that certain things in life are not available to us. It's as if our minds become blind to the things that exist outside of our reality.*

Two neuroscientists, David Hubel and Torsten Wiesel, conducted an experiment in which they divided a litter of newborn kittens, placing one half in an environment consisting of only vertical lines, and the other in an environment consisting of only horizontal lines. They took great care to ensure the kittens saw nothing but their designated lines, even coordinating the wallpaper, flooring, ceilings, and clothing of the people who fed them.

In the first few months of these kitten's lives they never experienced lines going the "other" way. When the kittens came out of their confined environments, they were blind – *literally blind* – to lines going the opposite way. The kittens from the horizontal group would bump into table legs because their brains couldn't physically compute vertical lines. The kittens from the vertical group would weave between the table legs but couldn't see the horizontal seat of the chair to jump up onto it.

This experiment shows just how malleable the mind is in those early stages. The lack of opposing information caused their minds to reject the possibility of something outside of their self-created reality and deny the *very real* lines going the other way.

> *Our beliefs become so strong that we will deny the possibility of anything that exceeds our perceived reality – be it unconditional love, safety, success, or anything else.*

The meaning we place on neutral information creates an invisible barrier that only exists in our minds. Just like those kittens, we won't even take the leap toward what we want if our reality doesn't support its existence.

Even the role we take in relationships is based on the meaning we assign to neutral information we collect as a child. In those early years our mother is our primary source of love, and therefore we see our father's role in the relationship as the best way to receive that love.

In his book *Professional Hypnotism Manual: Introducing Physical and Emotional Suggestibility and Sexuality*, John Kappas outlines that our sexual personality traits come from our interpretation of the secondary caretaker, which is usually the father.

John Kappas hypothesized that our sexual personality traits typically develop between ages eight to fourteen, and at a subconscious level we model our interpretation of our father figure as a way for us to get closer to the primary source of love (our mother).

The sexual personality traits can differ between siblings who grew up in the same home with the same parents because it's created based on the child's unique perception. This understanding sheds light on even more of our fabricated reality. Who you've become in relationships is based on the meaning you've placed on neutral information collected from your parents.

Each of us is experiencing life based on the meaning that we've assigned to neutral information. That meaning will influence everything from how we understand love and relationships to how we understand success and opportunity. If you grew up in a household where you lacked support and belief in your abilities, you may subconsciously come to the conclusion that certain things in life are unattainable simply because that was the meaning you placed on the information available.

Whereas if you grew up in a household where you felt supported and that influential people believed in you, you may subconsciously come to the conclusion that most things in life *are* attainable simply because that was the meaning you placed on the information available.

> *Support or lack of support is neutral information, it doesn't actually mean anything about you, it's simply the projection of the person giving it (or lacking it). You have the same potential regardless, but your actions will be determined by what you believe about yourself.*

As you move through life, you become exposed to new perspectives and new information which may ultimately oppose your beliefs and contradict that Illusion of Limitation. This creates an amazing opportunity for change. If a gap forms between your beliefs and new information, it provides you with an opportunity to change the meaning you've assigned to neutral information in your subconscious – a huge light bulb moment where you start to see things differently.

This is exactly what happened to me on that misty August morning. Something in that book challenged the beliefs I held about myself and what I was capable of. In that moment, the meaning I had assigned to neutral information from my experiences was opposed by this new understanding. This was enough to crack my Illusion of Limitation. It was a realization that the things I wanted only *seemed* out of reach. It gave me the courage to reach for those things that I'd previously felt were unattainable.

Little by little I began to open myself up to new experiences and step into unchartered territory because *I believed that I could*. Traveling and seeing the world was something that had always intrigued me as a kid. I remember flipping through the pages of our atlases and encyclopedias in amazement at the vastness of our world. I dreamed of seeing those faraway places but traveling on that scale exceeded the limits of my reality and felt completely unrealistic.

The fact that I perceived traveling as *unrealistic* impacted my choices when I went out into the world and had the opportunity to travel. Instead of spending money on traveling, I spent it on things that felt more realistic based on that Illusion of Limitation. Deep down, travel still sparked interest, but I didn't act upon that desire because I had unknowingly created a belief that it was out of reach.

Before I'd had that lightbulb moment, my husband and I had been on two international trips: one to Mexico, and then on our honeymoon to Hawaii. Even after *actually doing the thing I wanted so bad*, I still carried the belief that it wasn't "realistic" to spend my money on traveling and seeing the world.

After the Illusion of Limitation started to crack, I realized my perception of reality was holding me back in so many ways. In 2017, after giving birth to our second child, I decided I really did want to see the world and travel; I wanted to go to Europe. Simply bringing it up with my husband felt so strange, like I was proposing something so outrageous and unreasonable. His response was that we could plan a trip to Europe when our kids were older and we had more time ... *like retirement!*

I realized in that moment that he held the same limiting perception that I had about this desire. Traveling across the world felt unrealistic and not only did our subconscious conditioning make us feel that way, but we had also found ourselves in an environment that reinforced this belief. Nobody in our circle was traveling further than Mexico and, in fact, besides my mom's tales of backpacking through Europe, I didn't even know anybody who had traveled so far away. I had surrounded myself with people who reinforced my limiting beliefs by mirroring them.

I had always wanted to travel, and when I finally had the freedom to do it, I hesitated because those desires exceeded that Illusion of Limitation. I was perfectly capable of traveling just as those kittens were perfectly capable of making the leap to the seat of the chair, and yet the Illusion of Limitation kept me from ever booking a trip.

> *When we reach the edge of our reality and start to step across the threshold into something bigger, there is a voice that will tell us we can't do it. It's the voice of those deeply rooted beliefs and conditioning that's trying to keep us within that imaginary boundary.*

How could it be that we have hopes and dreams for ourselves and yet the Illusion of Limitation causes us to feel like it's completely out of reach? I've worked with countless business owners who have the desire to expand and evolve their business, yet they can't make it happen because the Illusion of Limitation is holding them back. They can look around and see other people creating the business that they want, yet still face massive resistance to creating it themselves.

Lina, for example, is a Brand Strategist and Designer who was building her dream business when she found herself hitting that wall of resistance. She had started her business and wanted to expand, but something about that goal was exceeding her Illusion of Limitation. Any time she had the opportunity to grow and expand her business she would find herself overanalyzing, stalling, and becoming derailed by worry and fear. Lina was great at her job and extremely passionate with such potential, and yet the Illusion of Limitation was making it impossible to grow.

Jesse was in a similar situation, at 60 she wanted a complete career change; she wanted to open an online marketing firm. This new career was exciting and everything she'd dreamed of, and yet when it came down to doing the things that she needed to do to create it, she found herself procrastinating and becoming completely unmotivated. She deeply desired this change but couldn't get through the Illusion of Limitation to make it happen.

The Illusion of Limitation causes us to settle for what's comfortable and familiar instead of going after what we really want. We become kennel-trained dogs. Deep down no dog is happy in their kennel, they want to explore, run around, and socialize. But they've been trained to see the kennel as safe and familiar. Just like those kennel-trained dogs, we've been conditioned to believe that whatever we've already created for ourselves is safer than what we truly desire.

> 66 *We've been conditioned to believe that anything outside the 'kennel' is not accessible. The only*

> *difference between the kennel-trained dog and you is that the dog is actually locked in, but you are not. Your kennel is imaginary, and you can cross the boundary at any time.* 🙰

My life changed forever when I realized that those perceived limitations didn't truly exist. A massive shift happened within me when I realized that I had been neglecting my deepest desires because they existed beyond that imaginary boundary.

Just like a kennel-trained dog, I had always yearned for *something more*, and for the first time in my life, I started to believe that it was actually possible.

> "There is no truth.
> There is only perception."
>
> GUSTAVE FLAUBERT

CHAPTER 2:

The Deception of Duality

There is a part of me that I would do anything to keep hidden. I would deny her existence because she made me feel insecure, awkward, and unworthy. I truly believed that if people ever saw this part of me, I would be rejected and humiliated.

Well into adulthood I was still struggling with the fear of judgment. I would get so twisted up in my head, creating stories about what people wouldn't like about me or how they would judge me if they *really* saw me.

This constant worry influenced a lot of my actions. I would hold myself to unrealistic standards, create strict, arbitrary timelines, and bend over backwards to be what I thought people wanted me to be. I was desperate to be liked because deep down I didn't like myself. I always felt judged because *I was judging myself.*

It's taken many years to finally understand why I feel this way, and it all comes back to that girl I would do anything to hide.

She's twelve years old with a messy low ponytail, a big gummy smile filled with braces and baggy sweatpants topped with a half-zipped hoodie. She looks slouchy and acts goofy. Just picturing this part of me made me cringe.

That's how I saw myself. That's the part of me that I would do anything to hide, mask, and deny. I was rejecting her because I felt like she was completely unlovable and unacceptable; a part of me that I felt ashamed of.

But it wasn't always this way. I didn't always hate parts of myself. As I worked with others through Hypnotherapy, I began to understand why this particular part of me was so hard to accept. It's a pattern that I see again and again with others.

I believe that when we come into this world, we are the rawest expression of ourselves. We are completely unashamed and unapologetic about who we are. However, this raw expression is at odds with our greatest need, our need for connection.

The highest level of connection is love. At its core, feeling loved is feeling deeply seen and accepted by another person. It's our instinctual nature to prioritize being loved above all else. As a vulnerable child, being unloved could mean our basic needs are neglected, which could ultimately lead to death. Even more so, our survival as a species is dependent upon community and our connection to others. Subconsciously, we are wired to value love and connection above all else, and our survival instincts will reinforce this belief.

However, love is not always available. If we don't feel like we can receive connection through its highest form of love, then we will seek connection through acceptance or attention of any kind. As we continue to interact with the world around us, seeking love and connection, we may perceive love as something that can be given and taken away. We may form an understanding that love is something that is conditional, for example: I am loved when I am quiet and obedient; I am unloved when I use my voice. Or perhaps, I am loved when I am strong; I am unloved when I am vulnerable and have needs.

We start to become aware that certain parts of our raw expression elicit more love than others. In essence, we are either perceiving a green light from others that tells us, 'Yes, this part of you is acceptable and yields love and connection' or a red light that means 'No, this part of you is unacceptable and yields pain and rejection.'

> *However, the map is not the territory. Our perception of rejection is not necessarily rejection; it is a negative interpretation of neutral information. As a child, we don't have the capacity to analyze our feelings; we simply believe them. If a child feels bad, then to them, it means that they are bad, and their minds will try to come up with a reason why.*

We are wired to avoid pain – both physical and psychological. For example, if you put your finger over a flame, the heat will cause physical pain and your subconscious mind will create a negative association to that experience so that in the future you are less likely to put your finger over a flame again. You create a belief that tells you that putting your finger over a flame causes pain.

However, your subconscious mind learns just as quickly from psychological pain. If you do something that causes psychological pain, such as rejection or shame, your subconscious mind will create a negative association to that experience so that in the future you are less likely to do the thing that caused the emotional pain.

For example, a child who receives love and connection for being quiet and obedient may interpret that as a "green light", creating positive associations to those qualities within herself. This same child may also feel rejected for being loud or outspoken, and therefore interpret that as a "red light", creating a negative association to those qualities. Over time, these red lights and green lights may cause her to believe that only certain qualities within her are loved and accepted. She may begin to "be" quiet or obedient out of her need for connection and fear of rejection. Eventually she may even feel uncomfortable being outspoken or disobedient regardless of the context because her subconscious has created a belief that those qualities will lead to pain.

The opposite could also be true. Another child may have felt neglected or ignored while being quiet and obedient and may have interpreted that as a "red light", creating a negative association to those qualities. This same child may have received a lot of attention (whether positive or negative) for being defiant or outspoken, and therefore interpreted that as a "green light" because even negative attention is still connection. Over time, these red lights and green lights may cause her to believe that certain qualities within her are more loved and accepted than others. She may begin to "be" defiant and outspoken out of a need for connection and fear of rejection.

We are not aware that we are creating negative associations to parts of ourselves when we get those red lights, the negative associations happen on a subconscious level. Consciously, we simply believe that parts of us are lovable and acceptable and other parts are not.

This understanding is not the absolute truth. It's the understanding we've come to accept based on our interpretation of neutral information. It's a subjective truth that becomes a core belief.

All through childhood we will seek green lights and avoid red lights. We collect neutral information from our parents, peers, and influential people to continue to form an understanding of our acceptable and unacceptable parts. More and more we lean into the parts of us that elicit love and connection and hide or sacrifice the parts of us that we believe will lead to pain and rejection.

This process of leaning into the parts of us that we believe are lovable, and rejecting the parts of us that we believe are unlovable, begins to create the Illusion of Duality.

> *The Illusion of Duality tells us that parts of us are 'good', and other parts of us are 'bad'. This illusion tricks us into thinking that we will be rejected if we allow the 'bad' parts of us to be seen. Because of this, we will do everything in our power to hide, reject, and deny those unlovable, unacceptable parts of us.*

This Illusion of Duality causes an internal conflict because the parts of us that we are denying and rejecting are fundamental parts of who we are. No matter how much we deny or reject those parts of ourselves, they still exist. And often, they still come out.

When I was about four years old, I made a lifelong friend. We instantly became *best friends*. We did everything together. As we grew up, I would see her every day at school, then immediately call her when I got home and talk for several more hours on the phone. We were inseparable.

Growing up I collected neutral information from my parents, peers and environment and came to conclusions as to what my most lovable (and most unlovable) parts were. Just like with most kids, there were parts of me that I was insecure about, and parts of me that I was proud of. Already,

I was coming to the conclusion that to be loved and accepted I had to lean into those "good" qualities and stray from those "bad" qualities.

The summer before middle school this tightly woven friendship abruptly ended. This hit me harder than I could ever have imagined; it was the biggest rejection I'd ever faced. I didn't realize it then, but the ending of that friendship made me believe that there was something deeply wrong with me. I was being rejected by one of the few people who knew me better than anyone else. It made me believe that those parts of me that I'd already decided were "bad" were completely unacceptable and unlovable. This experience caused me to subconsciously believe that nobody could ever truly love or accept the real me.

That part of me that I'd do anything to hide; it's her.

I moved into middle school with nobody. I was scared and alone and began to hide and mask the parts of myself that I believed caused that painful rejection. I would sacrifice any part of me just to feel connection with my peers and in the process, completely abandoned myself.

I was desperate to make new friends, and I did, but under the surface, the Illusion of Duality was more real than ever. I continued to see parts of myself as fundamentally flawed. Subconsciously, I tried to hide and deny the parts of me that I believed were the most unlovable.

> *I struggled with confidence because I was terrified of letting those unlovable parts of me be seen. I became highly sensitive to the way others would react to me because my subconscious was always looking for reasons why I felt rejected.*

I struggled in friendships; always feeling judged by the people I would let in because I believed nobody could ever love or accept the real me – pushing people away when they got close. I was constantly on edge, assigning meaning to neutral information that reinforced my subconscious beliefs. That fear was always lingering in the background, telling me that nobody would accept the real me – I had to keep her hidden.

This is not the story of a villain and a victim, but rather the perfect depiction of the Illusion of Duality at play. The friendship served as neutral information in which I created meaning. The divide that occurred between myself and this friend did not objectively indicate anything wrong with me. It was my interpretation of this experience, along with what I already deemed was "wrong with me" that caused me to succumb to this illusion.

> *Relationships in any form, whether platonic or romantic, serve as neutral information in which we use to create meaning about ourselves. Highly influential people, especially in those early years, will have a larger impact on the beliefs we construct and the illusions we believe.*

I see this same pattern showing up in different ways in a lot of individuals. The Illusion of Duality causes them to see part of themselves as bad or unacceptable so, out of fear of being rejected by others, they will deny, mask, or try to hide those parts of themselves.

The illusion goes undetected because they simply see those parts of them as embarrassing, shameful, or unlikable. Yet they still exist. Our denial of their existence causes us more pain. This is exactly what Darcy was going through when we met.

Darcy contacted me after an incident at her workplace had triggered an extreme emotional reaction that continued for weeks. She was feeling so much anxiety that she took time off work and isolated herself in her home. When we started sessions, we soon found that the incident at work had only triggered a much deeper wound that she'd been carrying for most of her life.

After guiding her into a trance state, I prompted her subconscious to follow the emotion that the workplace incident caused her to feel. She was immediately brought back to an early childhood memory. In this early memory she was upset and crying, needing comfort from her mother. However, her mother was busy with her other children and didn't respond to her cries. This was neutral information that Darcy used to create meaning. In those vulnerable moments, she felt deeply rejected. Without the ability to logically analyze this experience, Darcy internalized the rejection and created an understanding that being vulnerable would cause her pain. Being the youngest in a big family, she felt that her emotional sensitivity made her a burden to her mother. Unconsciously, she began to disown and reject the emotional, vulnerable part of her as a sacrifice in order to receive love and connection from her mother.

From that early experience, she continued to unconsciously deny this emotional, sensitive part of her to the point of being almost completely cut off from her emotions. She perceived her emotional sensitivity as a weakness, and something to be ashamed of. The emotional, sensitive, and vulnerable part of her was a fundamental part of who she was. Denying this part of her was leading to even more pain and suffering. The reason that the workplace incident caused her such a massive amount of anxiety was because it had triggered this deeper unhealed wound. Accepting the parts of her that she deemed so unacceptable was the only way for her to move forward.

There are many reasons why a person would reject parts of themselves. In some cases, like Darcy's experience, we reject parts of ourselves as a sacrifice in order to receive love and connection. Other times, such as my experience, our self-rejection is a mirror for what we believe others have rejected in us. And then there are times when we reject parts of ourselves due to trauma we've experienced.

> *Traumatic experiences can cause us to reject parts of ourselves because we believe that those parts of us are the reason for the trauma. This can cause a person to begin to reject and deny fundamental parts of themselves such as their independence, their voice, or their sexuality.*

Another client of mine, Vanessa, struggled with confidence and self-sacrificing patterns. This subconscious conditioning caused her to take a back seat in her own life for many years. She spent a large portion of adulthood in a relationship that was keeping her small, sacrificing her biggest dreams for her partner's happiness, and being afraid to be fully seen in her own business.

In our session, I guided Vanessa into a trance state and prompted her subconscious to get to the root cause of that pattern. She was brought back to early memories where she was subjected to a verbally abusive parent. In the memories she was scolded for speaking up or being disobedient, which caused her to create negative associations to those qualities within herself. From that early age, she internalized her feelings and used them to create an understanding that acting assertively or using her voice would cause her pain.

Over time this caused her to unconsciously reject the assertive, defiant parts of her that were constantly getting red lights from her parent. Vanessa contacted me because she realized that she felt unable to voice what she wanted in her relationships and in her life. She had dreams for her future, but she would continue to sacrifice her desires out of a fear of rejection from those she loved most.

The Illusion of Duality held her back because she deemed fundamental parts of herself as "bad" and unconsciously believed that if she were to speak up and voice her needs it would cause her to face the same deep rejection as it had earlier in life.

I realized that, just like Vanessa, I too had been rejecting parts of myself due to trauma I had experienced. Years earlier I experienced sexual trauma that caused me to feel deep shame and fear. I didn't realize it until much later that I was unconsciously rejecting parts of my sexuality due to the shame that I still carried from that experience. Consciously I knew that my sexuality wasn't something to be ashamed of, but, deep down, feelings of shame would creep in and overshadow part of my life.

It wasn't until years after my trauma that I realized I'd been carrying this sexual shame – I thought the feelings I felt were normal. That's how these rejected parts of us continue to go undetected. It's not until we start to consciously question our conditioning that we even have the opportunity to understand what's happening on a subconscious level. Often we don't even realize that we are rejecting parts of us. It's so seamlessly woven into our experience that we just see those parts of us as undesirable. It's common to also reject these self-rejected qualities in others too, leading to anger, jealousy or resentment.

> *We project that Illusion of Duality onto others and deem them as bad or unacceptable simply because they display the qualities that we cannot accept within ourselves. We become triggered when we witness somebody else embodying the qualities that we've been denying ourselves of.*

I noticed this happening in my own life. Certain people or behaviors would elicit a feeling of jealously or resentment within me, causing me to act defensive, cold, or spiteful. Exploring the rejected parts of me made me realize that the parts of *them* that triggered me the most were actually the parts of *me* that I was denying. I was rejecting these parts of myself, so witnessing others embody them made me feel angry or jealous because I wasn't allowing myself to embody them, too. The reason I felt triggered was because those qualities also exist within me.

Shattering the Illusion of Duality requires us to see that there is no duality at all. There are no good or bad parts of us, that is simply the meaning we've assigned to neutral information. Until we understand this, we will continue to believe that we need to hide or reject parts of our raw expression, leading to shame, insecurity and unworthiness. This illusion will create a wedge between our rawest expression and who we allow ourselves to be. The further we push ourselves away from who we really are, the more dissatisfying our lives become.

"Trauma compromises our ability to engage with others by replacing patterns of connection with patterns of protection"

STEPHEN PORGES

CHAPTER 3:

Internally Unsafe

The woman across from me shut her eyes and went quiet.

My heart felt like it was going to beat out of my chest. I could feel a wave of emotion coming up as I tried to sit still. My body was getting hot and my hands felt clammy and shaky. We were in class together and had been paired up for a body scan. She was very gifted, and I was extremely fearful of what she might see.

She furrowed her brows and made a face like she was trying to understand; my stomach grew knots. I knew what she saw, and it terrified me.

After a moment she opened her eyes and began to speak. I wanted to run.

"I noticed a black spot ..." she said, gesturing her hand over her lower abdomen, right at her ovaries.

I couldn't keep it in. I wanted to run but I couldn't move. The tears started trailing down my cheeks and I could feel my lips quiver. I couldn't speak. All I could do was stare into her eyes. It felt like a dream, like a nightmare.

If I would have known that I was about to face the deepest, darkest part of me, there's no way I would've come here. I'd never stopped running from this; I never wanted to face it. But this was it. I couldn't run anymore.

Early March in 2018 I was scrolling Facebook when I came across a training class for something called Theta Healing. I didn't know what it was, but something in me lit up.

I began to read the description of the training and felt an insane urge to attend. I'd never heard of Theta Healing before, nor had I ever taken a training class quite like it. As I read on, I learned that Theta Healing is a method for healing and personal growth based on Hypnotherapy principles. At this point I hadn't taken any Hypnotherapy training – it hadn't even entered my radar yet, but I was very intrigued. I registered for the event without a second thought. I just felt certain I needed to be there.

Looking back, I know that attending this weekend class changed me. For the first time ever, I came face to face with my deepest trauma and finally started to heal from my sexual abuse. After years of running from it, I finally sat with it. I realized something profound that weekend; I realized that the harder I ran from that part of me, the scarier it felt. The more I denied it, the heavier it became.

You can't run from something in your mind. You can't hide from it, deny it, or stuff it down. In fact, the more you try to push it away, the more threatening it becomes. I didn't know that back then. I thought I was keeping myself safe. I thought if I just "stay strong", I could outrun it. I didn't know I was creating my own hell.

Trauma creates physical changes in the brain. Childhood trauma is especially impactful because your brain is still developing. When you experience early life trauma it changes parts of your brain called the hypothalamus and the amygdala, which are responsible for producing oxytocin and for emotional regulation. Trauma in those early years dysregulates your system as it's developing.

Ultimately, this change impacts how you regulate your emotions and how you handle stress. The impact from stress and trauma early in life can continue to affect you all through adulthood. In those early years we are creating our perception of reality and any early life stress throws a wrench into it. It distorts our perception of self and how we experience the world around us.

> *Varying degrees of childhood trauma can lead to a whole host of what I would call 'symptoms', such as depression, anxiety, a lack of self-esteem, codependency, even physical pain and disease.*

That early life stress is stored. Your subconscious holds the memories and, most importantly, the emotion of that trauma. It lies just below the surface, affecting how you think, feel, and behave. The more you deny it, the more it manifests.

The distortion from that trauma creates an Illusion of Unsafety that is woven into your realm of reality. It affects the way you see yourself and the way you interact with the world around you. It creates the illusion of danger when danger may not be present.

The effects of trauma can find its way into many parts of your life. It's like dumping a tank of oil into the ocean. It doesn't stay in the area where it was dumped. It moves and flows into different areas, spreading so thin you almost can't tell where it is and where it isn't.

I used to think my sexual trauma didn't affect me. I was managing fine, I hadn't turned to drugs or alcohol, I hadn't gotten into abusive relationships or had a hard time holding down a job. I thought I was unscathed. I didn't realize it was actually everywhere. It seeped into so many parts of me I couldn't tell where it was and where it wasn't. It came out in my thoughts, it influenced my emotions, and it impacted my actions and decisions. It had been there so long that for me, it felt normal.

I thought the tension I felt was normal. I thought the fear and shame I felt was normal. I thought the painful flashbacks and intrusive thoughts I experienced were normal. I thought the way I saw myself was normal because that was the reality I had been living for years.

What was really happening was that I was reliving that trauma over and over. My nervous system was experiencing that same stress each time my environment triggered that fearful feeling. I was experiencing the world through the Illusion of Unsafety. At times the emotional reaction I would feel would be out of proportion to what was actually happening. Fear, panic, shame, or anger would sweep over me in completely non-threatening moments.

When you experience something traumatic or highly distressing, your subconscious mind keeps track of the details of that experience. It closely documents how you felt, where you were, what you saw, the sounds, the smells, and any feeling associated with that experience. Ultimately, your brain wants to avoid the stress of that experience from happening again. This is a primal response to stress – create negative associations so that in the future the stress can be avoided.

But the problem is you might be in a safe, non-threatening environment when your subconscious mind becomes triggered. It could be a sound, smell or even another person's behavior that tips off those negative associations and sounds your internal stress alarm. You may begin to experience emotions or stress in your body, similar to the stress you experienced during the initial experience, sending your body into a fight, flight, freeze or fawn response.

Within seconds, the amygdala detects a threat and sends a signal to the hypothalamus which communicates to the body through the autonomic nervous system. The hypothalamus signals the adrenal glands to pump adrenaline to the bloodstream causing the nervous system's sympathetic response. The sympathetic response is the "stress response" and affects over a dozen different systems in your body, from cortisol secretion to pupil dilation and more.

> *You may not even know what triggered the stress response consciously – or that you were triggered at all, and suddenly you experience a wave of panic, fear, shame or anger sweep over you. You might feel your heart rate begin to increase, or it might feel like intense emotion comes out of nowhere. Your body is preparing to face a threat that may not even exist.*

For some, this happens all the time and is completely debilitating. This is the definition of an anxiety disorder. According to the Mayo Clinic, people who suffer an anxiety disorder "frequently have intense, excessive, and persistent worry and fear about everyday situations. Often, anxiety disorders involve repeated episodes of sudden feelings of intense anxiety and fear or terror that reach a peak within minutes (panic attacks). These feelings of anxiety and panic interfere with daily activities, are difficult to control, are out of proportion to the actual danger and can last a long time."

The intense fear and anxiety are simply symptoms of unresolved emotion that become unconsciously triggered in day-to-day life. I have people tell me all the time, "I don't have trauma; I had a great childhood." But trauma comes in many forms. It doesn't always show up as abuse, neglect, or violence.

Trauma can be categorized as big "T" or little "t" trauma. Big "T" traumas are experiences that are commonly associated with post-traumatic stress disorder such as serious injury, physical or sexual abuse, deaths, or events that were life-threatening. Little "t" traumas are experiences that were highly distressing on a personal level but don't fall into the big "T" category. These types of traumas are often overlooked because they may not appear traumatic to anyone but the person experiencing it. This could include emotional abuse, verbal abuse, harassment, or loss of any kind.

Just like big "T" trauma, we store the emotion from little "t" trauma, and it can continue to affect us long after the event happened. With little "t" trauma it's even typical for the experience itself to be forgotten, but the unprocessed emotion that is tied to the memory remains in the subconscious mind.

When you have unprocessed emotion from a past experience, it can cause exaggerated emotions, commonly showing up as fear, shame, or anger. It's as if that emotion lies just below the surface, being triggered by everyday life occurrences.

You may experience exaggerated fear, as associated with anxiety, or you may experience it differently. Maybe it comes out as anger instead. Your reaction to everyday annoyances may seem over the top. Or perhaps the feeling of shame runs deep for you. It may even hold you back from being intimate with a partner, advancing in your career, taking the next step in life; even leading to depression.

The Illusion of Unsafety prevails because in some cases we don't even realize our emotions are out of proportion. We may not realize we are experiencing unprocessed emotions which are exaggerated due to past experiences.

> *The effects of trauma can seep into all areas of our lives without us noticing, because our perception has been distorted. When those unprocessed emotions are triggered, we lose access to logical thinking and our body simply reacts.*

This was the case for Aria. Aria had a history of anxiety and at the time we met she was experiencing extreme fear when dropping her son off at school. Some days the fear became so severe she would even consider keeping him home. The anxiety of the almost daily task of school drop-off would send a ripple effect into her day. Over and over, she would endure the fear and anxiety without understanding where it was coming from or how to resolve it.

We focused on releasing the fear connected to school drop-off. In our session I guided her subconscious to reveal the root cause of the fear and she was brought back to a traumatic childhood memory that she had suppressed for decades. In this experience, she was overwhelmed with fear and felt extremely unsafe due to the actions of someone she trusted. That unsafe feeling had been internalized. This event shifted the way she experienced life by creating the Illusion of Unsafety, affecting her throughout her life by causing her to feel unsafe in non-threatening environments.

That unsafe feeling was being triggered by everyday occurrences since that distressing event, causing unproportioned anxiety to non-threatening experiences. The intense fear she felt at school drop-off was connected to the fear from earlier in life – her body was simply reacting to the unprocessed fear that had been stored in her subconscious mind.

It doesn't always take a big "T" trauma to cause the Illusion of Unsafety. Little "t" traumas and stress in early life can build up to create a feeling of unsafety.

Claire had struggled with anxiety all her life. When she contacted me, it was showing up in her relationship as a fear of being rejected and abandoned. If there was a lack of communication or if her partner wasn't reassuring her of his love, the anxiety would ramp up and cause her to think he would abandon her. This anxiety would get so intense that she would cancel work meetings and isolate herself completely.

In our session, I guided Claire into a trance state and prompted her subconscious to show her the root cause of the anxiety. She was taken back to an early childhood memory of sitting up in bed in the middle of the night, scared and unable to sleep. In this early memory she had gone to her mother's room for comfort and reassurance, but her mother had sent her back to bed. So there she sat, anxious and afraid.

In that early memory she believed that being alone was unsafe. This almost exactly mirrored the feelings she was struggling with in her relationship. Unless her partner was constantly reassuring her, she felt anxious and afraid. That fear had remained with her for decades, becoming triggered by completely non-threatening experiences.

The longer we run, the scarier it becomes. Facing our own trauma may just be the scariest thing we do. So scary in fact, most of us won't do it. Most of us will keep running because it seems like running will keep us safe. It seems like stuffing it down or denying it will protect us. Facing my own trauma was the scariest thing I'd ever done, and yet it was the only way out.

I didn't realize just how heavy it had become. I didn't realize how much that unprocessed emotion was affecting me until I released it. It felt like a hundred pounds was lifted off my shoulders. It felt like I could take a deep breath and relax parts of me that had been tense for years.

I understand what it feels like to carry that burden, and I know what it feels like to finally put it down. It wasn't until the Theta Healing weekend that I realized how much of a hold my past had on me, and how much things could change in an instant.

And this is the beauty of the mind.

> *Your brain has the ability to change and adapt; this is referred to as neuroplasticity. This means that even the trauma and early life stress that altered your brain chemistry can shift.*

The neuropathways in your mind that cause the Illusion of Unsafety can change, and the distortion that your trauma has created can evaporate. I regularly have people tell me that facing and healing their deepest trauma changed their life. How can releasing a lifetime of stored emotion not change your life? It changes everything.

Releasing the stored emotion resolves the triggers because the triggers are a manifestation of the unprocessed emotion. Healing suppressed emotion dramatically increases the quality of life because the buildup of emotion is gone. Your capacity to experience emotion without feeling overwhelmed is increased. You no longer need to rely on your coping mechanisms to feel safe and in control.

Most importantly, when you heal the unprocessed emotion that was caused by distressing events from your past, you shatter the Illusion of Unsafety. Without the illusion distorting your perception of reality, many things that used to feel dangerous or threatening become accessible and attainable.

"When you shut down emotion, you're also affecting your immune system, your nervous system. So the repression of emotion, which is a survival strategy, then becomes a source of physiological illness later on."

GABOR MATÉ

CHAPTER 4:

Separation Breeds Suffering

I was fifteen years old, jogging up the gravel road every day with my dog, Rex.

Rex was like one of the kids, he'd been a part of the family since I was five. Together we would jog up the road and back, about two kilometers, every day. He always came with me. It had been nearly a month straight when I started to notice Rex would fall way behind. Then he would only come a little way with me. Then he would only come a few paces out of the driveway and head back.

I was angry. He was supposed to come with me. What if I ran into a wild animal? There were no houses down this road, just fields on one side and forest on the other. How could he do this to me? Why would he abandon me? I would call for him, but he wouldn't come.

One evening while the family and I were watching television we heard noises coming from Rex's bed. He took a few really deep breaths, and then he never took another.

He was gone.

I was devastated; a lifelong friend just gone. The sadness was overwhelming, but the guilt was worse. I had pushed him every day to come with me on the run. I didn't know he wasn't well. I didn't know those were his final days. I carried so much guilt over his death, feeling like somehow it was my fault, like I'd pushed him too far.

It took me weeks, but I eventually started running again. Within a very short time I was unable to run from the sharp pains in my hips. The pain first showed up only on my runs, but soon the pain was nearly constant. It became so severe that I had trouble just lifting my legs to pull pants on each morning. It was painful to walk or even stand for long periods of time. It was diagnosed as bursitis, a condition where the small fluid-filled sacs that cushion the bones near the joint become inflamed.

My doctor said I should rest and it would heal in a matter of weeks. I quit running but even after weeks of rest the bursitis would flare up if I did anything too strenuous. Months turned to years and still any amount of standing or walking would cause pain and swelling. The pain in my hips was constant.

I didn't understand the mind-body connection back then. I felt like my body had failed me, like it was weak and fragile. I felt helpless to fix my hips or heal the pain.

The connection between mind and body is easy to see when we get excited and feel butterflies in our stomach or get anxious and feel tension in our chest – the effect is immediate. But the truth is, this connection between mind and body is happening constantly, and over time can have a tremendous effect on our bodies. We're living in a time where the Illusion of Separateness between the mind and body is causing suffering on so many levels.

> *The mind and body are completely entangled. The body is a physical extension of the mind, and the mind is a metaphysical extension of the body. They are two parts of the same system; what happens in one will ultimately affect the other.*

The mind is not the brain; the mind exists within the entire body. There is an intelligence that exists in every cell working simultaneously with the mind. The placebo effect is an excellent example of this intelligence.

If your mind believes a pill or treatment will heal your body, then there is a large probability that it will; even if it's just a sugar pill. When the mind believes, the intelligence in the body will begin to heal just as the mind believes it should. Placebos seem to have an effect on almost every symptom known to man, and work in at least a third of patients. In fact, it's not uncommon for the placebo to be nearly as effective as the drug it's being tested against.

The placebo effect isn't just for sugar pills. One of the most incredible placebo experiments was Dr. Bruce Moseley's placebo knee surgeries. Dr. Moseley divided a group of 180 patients suffering from severe knee pain in half, giving one group real arthroscopy surgery on their knees, and the other group a placebo surgery. Patients in the placebo group were given anesthesia and a small incision on their knee but no repairs to the damaged cartilage or clearing out any loose bone fragments took place. To add to the illusion, the doctors and nurses talked through a real surgery even while performing the placebo surgery.

The results were staggering. There was no measurable difference between the group that received the real surgery and the group that received the placebo. All patients reported a decrease in frequency, intensity, and duration of knee pain.

> *The power of the mind-body connection is extremely under-stated. The placebo effect has been used in thousands of studies over the last several hundred years, proving again and again that our minds and bodies are completely intertwined.*

In 2019 I was going through a very stressful time. My husband and I were in the process of leaving our company, selling our shares to a business partner, and things got a little messy. If I'm honest, they got a lot messy. At that time, it was the most stress I had ever been under.

The stress of leaving the business came down to one thing for me: my worth. My experience was the partnership of a dominating male figure that did not see my worth as a business partner for the three years we were in business together and was confronted with it when I sold my shares and left the business. The dispute was about money as it usually is in business, but for me the dispute was really about my value.

During the months of back and forth, I was absolutely overcome with emotion as I felt wronged by someone that I had trusted. I felt powerless.

About three months into this stressful time I started to feel like something was wrong. I was having dull pains in my lower abdomen, and it was starting to worry me. One day, after a few weeks of on and off again pain, it started to get really bad. Within a few minutes the dull pain went from a hardly noticeable discomfort to a 10/10 sharp pain. I winced and held my lower abdomen but just as fast as the pain ramped up, it was gone.

It almost made me question if the pain was ever there in the first place – until it happened again a few days later. I was panicked by this point, thinking that something was seriously wrong. I made a doctor's appointment and as it turned out, the pain was caused by ovarian cysts, which are not uncommon, and also, not fatal. It was odd to have these cysts come out of nowhere; I'd never had issues like this before. However, by this time I had come to learn a bit about the mind-body connection.

I'm a big fan of Louise Hay's work, and in the self-development world, she's a bit of a celebrity. She wrote a book called *You Can Heal Your Life*, in which she outlines the probable link between emotional issues and physical symptoms in the body. I also have another, much larger book called *Metaphysical Anatomy* by Evette Rose that acts like a dictionary for any ailment or symptom that you could possibly have, with the corresponding probable emotional connection.

> *The mind-body approach sees the body as a mirror. The body is creating a physical manifestation that mirrors the emotional experience.*

I've witnessed the accuracy of this theory by looking up my own ailments and reading about the emotional connection.

I'm not surprised that I developed physical symptoms during those months because the stress was all consuming, but why in my ovaries? I thought back to the Theta Healing weekend when the woman described the black spot in my lower abdomen. Perhaps the trauma from my past had caused a weak spot? Or perhaps the feelings I felt from my sexual trauma were similar to the feelings I felt as this business deal went south.

I felt chills as I read the interpretation of ovarian cysts according to *Metaphysical Anatomy*:

"You may be consumed by the unjust treatment and behavior of others … You don't feel that you are permitted to put a stop to people's behavior, which is upsetting you. You may have been made to believe that women have to obey, listen and always compromise for the sake of other's needs – emotional, physical or intimate. You are rebelling against projections and expectations from influential people and fighting off dominant figures."

Evette Rose, *Metaphysical Anatomy*, 558

The body is a mirror, and the ovaries were not a coincidence.

About eight months later the business deal was coming to a close, and as the stress began to fade, so did my symptoms. I experienced the last episode of cysts just a few weeks after the last bit of paperwork was signed and filed.

I found it very interesting (and a bit terrifying) to witness the physical manifestation of my emotional distress. It's almost like I hit the stress overload and it began to spill over into my physical body, which doesn't surprise me; I felt completely overwhelmed with stress. It was like a constant hum in the background of everything I did.

I would wake up with tension in the pit of my stomach. The daily tasks and activities were a distraction from the thoughts but the tightness in my body never really left. As soon as I had time to let my mind wander – in the car on the way home; while eating lunch; lying in bed as I tried to fall asleep – my mind would immediately return to the stressful thoughts, and the tightening and physical discomfort would heighten.

It was more stress than I could manage. Not only that but, because the situation that caused the stress lasted eight months, I felt like there was no way out. The ways that I had previously managed stress were not working.

My autonomic nervous system had activated the sympathetic response (the stress response), and wouldn't turn off until I got to safety. The problem was, I couldn't get to safety. The threat was constant. It followed me everywhere, intruding into all parts of my day. Instead of living in the parasympathetic state where my body could relax and focus on regeneration and regulation, it had the alarm bells going off all hours of the day and night. My body was falling out of balance, and it took only a few weeks of this inner chaos to reach the breaking point where emotional imbalance turned into physical disease.

In my experience, the stress and physical symptoms were obvious. The pain started just a few weeks into the emotional distress and faded away just a few weeks after it all ended. The connection was easy to make but, in most cases, the dots never connect, and we experience aches, pains, and ailments that seem to happen at random.

I worked with Heather who, at the time, was struggling with anxiety and panic. It had reached a point where it was limiting many areas of her life and she knew she needed to go deeper to resolve it. After a few sessions we were able to release a lot of emotion that was stored in her subconscious and get to the root of the panic and anxiety.

She described this relief like a weight being lifted off her shoulders; she felt lighter, like she'd put down something heavy she'd been carrying for far too long. Interestingly enough, she noticed a weight being lifted physically as well. Prior to our sessions Heather had been seeing a chiropractor for regular adjustments because she held a lot of tension in her back. Her job was very physically demanding, and she assumed that the continual need for adjustments came from the physical stress that she endured at work.

However, when she released the emotional weight from her subconscious, she also released the unconscious tension in her back. There was a notable difference in her back after releasing the stored emotion from her subconscious; even her chiropractor commented on how easily she was adjusting and asked what she was doing different. Prior to the Hypnotherapy sessions she had been going to the chiropractor multiple times a week for adjustments. She now books in for monthly maintenance adjustments due to her work and exercise regime. Along with the relief of back pain, she also noticed an eye twitch that she'd had for years had completely disappeared.

This experience isn't uncommon in this work. Early in my work on chronic disease I worked with Tory, who suffered from a thyroid condition called Hashimoto's Disease, as well as many other ailments in her body. For a long time she had a big lump in her back that she had named Dave. Dave had been there for years, and she had never had relief from the pain and tension. Through our sessions working on the pain and symptoms related to her condition, we released a lot of stress that she was holding onto on a subconscious level. While we worked on releasing this internal stress, Dave quietly faded away. After a few weeks I asked about Dave and watched her eyes widen as she reached over her shoulder to where the lump had been. It was gone, along with many of her other symptoms.

It's clear that unchecked stress can lead to physical aches and pains, but there have been studies showing the link between early life stress and much more serious conditions. I can't emphasize enough the significance of the first few years of childhood and the effect that they have on the rest of your life. When those early years are tainted with things like abuse, neglect, parental depression, or other forms of household dysfunction it has a major effect on your developing nervous system.

> *When you are made to feel unsafe from an early age from unpredictable parents or threats to your physical safety, your nervous system is essentially put into high alert. This causes your body to function in a highly vigilant state where it feels danger or threats are around every corner. The perceived threat goes from 'out there' to 'in here' as we internalize the feeling of danger.*

When your autonomic nervous system gets stuck in the sympathetic response, changes to your body, like cortisol levels, blood sugar, insulin levels, blood pressure, heart rate and other physiological functions, get stuck at a dangerous rate.

In a study of over 38,000 participants, the link between early childhood stress and the development of autoimmune disease was clear. Participants who experienced just two or more adverse childhood experiences (ACE) were up to 80% more likely to develop an autoimmune disease. The risk then continues to climb for every adverse experience that you encounter, because your nervous system is already activating the stress response. As you go through life, stressful events like accidents, divorce or unemployment, can have a much larger impact on your nervous system because it already lacks the ability to self-regulate. That additional stress can cause even more pressure on your body, resulting in pain or dysfunction.

> *It appears that pain or disease comes 'out of nowhere', with seemingly no cause, but under the surface the emotional distress has been causing stress on your body all along, and finally hits the breaking point where the stress results in physical pain or bodily dysfunction.*

We are led to believe that our condition is incurable, that there is no clear cause; prolonging our suffering, strengthening the Illusion of Separateness and creating a greater disconnect from our bodies. But what happens when you crack the Illusion of Separateness and see your mind and body as two parts of the same system? What happens when you release the underlying emotional buildup of fear and create a sense of safety in the mind and body?

Pain disappears. Symptoms evaporate. Tension releases.

I worked with Casey, a young mother of two who suffered with chronic migraines. The migraines were so constant and severe they would cause her to miss out on time with her kids, social activities, and work. Over the years she had been to numerous doctors and specialists to try to determine the cause, with no success.

At the time we met, Casey was suffering with varying degrees of a migraine every single day. When we began to work on the deeper emotional cause of the migraines and started to release the stored emotion from her subconscious, the pattern of migraines began to shift. After just a handful of sessions her migraines had decreased from daily debilitating pain to about three migraines per month. When she released the emotional tension she had been holding in her subconscious mind, the physical tension in her body could finally release. Nearly three years later and the daily migraines have not returned.

> *As I have said, the mind and body are deeply intertwined. When we feel emotionally unsafe, that fear is mirrored in the body and shows up as tension and stress on our internal systems. The effects may be immediate, like a knot in your*

> *stomach or a shiver up your spine. Or it may take years for physical symptoms to appear with no clear connection between the mind and body.* 99

The Illusion of Separateness causes disempowerment and disconnection from our bodies. It causes us to believe that our bodies are weak and have failed us, or that we are powerless in our healing. This couldn't be further from the truth. Our minds are the most powerful tool for healing, and when we break the Illusion of Separateness, we realize that our bodies are a physical extension of our minds, there is no separation. We realize that the pain and symptoms we experience are messages from within. Instead of masking our symptoms and enduring the pain, we go within and *listen*.

Healing is a complex system and there is no one-size-fits-all solution. However, each of us has the ability to heal ourselves. Once we crack the Illusion of Separateness, we understand that true healing must occur in both the body *and mind*.

PART 2
THE HEALING

"Reality is merely an illusion, albeit a very persistent one."

ALBERT EINSTEIN

CHAPTER 5:

Crossing the Threshold

There's a little voice in our mind that stops us from doing crazy things.

You know, like jumping off a cliff, running out into traffic, speaking out against the norm, going after your dreams, being vulnerable in front of strangers – crazy stuff like that. It's that whisper from the back of your mind that tells you, *"This is dangerous."*

This little voice has one purpose: to keep us safe.

The problem is, even when there's mounting evidence proving that something is in fact safe, it sometimes feels impossible to take action if that little voice is yelling, *"Danger!"* That voice kicks in when you're about to do something that would cause you to stretch yourself past the point of comfort and into the unknown. This voice is the Illusion of Limitation and it perceives anything outside of your realm of reality as dangerous.

If we're not careful, we can buy into the illusion that this little voice is the *voice of truth*. We can be misled into believing that this voice is reality – *it isn't*. This little voice is not your higher self guiding you to greatness; it's your subconscious conditioning trying to keep you within the confines of your reality. It's the voice of caution that can inadvertently make your life *stale* in an attempt to make your life *safe*.

> **This voice will always prioritize the safety of the known and comfortable over doing anything that would risk rejection, failure, or pain. Over and over again, I was faced with this little voice as I broke out of my old realm of reality in an attempt to change my life.**

In late 2017 I had this crazy idea to become a Life Coach. I wanted to help people who were struggling like I had been – I know, it was completely nuts, and that little voice was going off the charts letting me know it was definitely *not* going to work out. In the early months of 2018, I signed up for Life Coach training and, although the little voice was still there, the excitement of this new adventure was far too distracting.

Then around the end of May I finished the training. You know what that means, right? I actually had to *be a Life Coach*.

Now all I could hear was the alarm bells ringing in my head and felt imminent danger as I approached the edge of my little reality. Reading books and taking training in the comfort of my home was fine, but that voice told me that, somehow, presenting myself to my peers as a Life Coach would surely be the end of me. It was a very *dangerous* idea.

However, I decided to push through and hit 'post' on the very official Instagram photo that said I was open for business. I could hardly believe it – I didn't die! Instead, I ended up signing up my first client.

I continued in this fashion for a few months, working with a client here and a client there, and then in about October of that year I started to hear that voice again. This time, it was letting me know that although I hadn't died from these poor decisions yet, this path would not lead me to the greener grass I was imagining.

This time, it was telling me that although I had worked with a few people here and there, this would never really work out.

I mean, who am I kidding, right? You think you can just wake up one day and decide to build a successful business? If it were that easy, everybody would be doing it. Plus, what do I really have to offer people? I'm just some girl. And just look around at the others, they seem to have almost immediate success, while I've only seen two or three clients. In fact, who's to say I've even helped these people? Who's to say I can really help anyone?

Clearly, I'm better off throwing in the towel now, and not continuing this embarrassing charade. And if I choose to continue, I'm sure to face humiliation, public shaming, and rejection from my closest friends and family. Or, at least, that's what the little voice wanted me to think.

I figured, if I've already tarnished my reputation this badly, I couldn't possibly do more damage.

Two weeks later I announced I would be hosting a workshop. That's right, I decided to announce that I would be hosting a *public* workshop to share some of the knowledge and information that I'd learned on my journey thus far.

Oh boy, did that send that little voice over the edge. This would *surely* be the end of me. Public speaking was *very* far outside of my little reality, and it felt *extremely* uncomfortable. Yet again I was approaching the edge of my realm of reality and the Illusion of Limitation was triggering immense fear.

> *The voice in your head is a protection mechanism against danger and threats. One step outside that realm of reality might as well be a leap off a cliff. Every time I got close to the edge, the Illusion of Limitation caused an immediate desire to retreat back to safety.*

That little voice had me so worked up that during the workshop, which I held in my living room, my hands wouldn't stop shaking, my mouth had somehow completely dried up, I couldn't make eye contact with anyone, and my thoughts were so scrambled I likely didn't make any sense at all. I even started the workshop without realizing one guest was in the washroom.

Without a doubt this was the worst decision I'd ever made. It was a complete failure, an embarrassment, and pretty much as bad as that voice told me it would be.

So I did it again, two weeks later.

This time, I rented a public space, and invited a dozen more people. I mean really, what's "public humiliation" if it isn't in public, right? In those two weeks I felt calm. I was too busy preparing for the workshop to notice the shitstorm that was brewing in the back of my mind.

The night before the workshop I was at my sister's house, going over the last-minute details when I started to feel an emotional tidal wave approaching.

Oh, *it was bad.*

It was full blown panic. There were tears, a knot in the pit of my stomach, and so much fear.

What the hell was I thinking? I'm not qualified to speak to people about anything. My notes are a mess, my slideshow looks like a toddler's coloring page, and my speaking points are shaky at best. What if I forget what to say? What if someone asks me a question? I can't answer questions. What if I can't even bring myself to speak? What if I break down in front of a room full of strangers? What are they going to think of me? How will I ever live this down? This is the stupidest thing I've ever done and there's no way out.

That little voice was right about one thing; there was no way out. Over a dozen people had purchased tickets and were expecting a workshop, so I had no choice. I had to pull myself together and try to make it through. The following evening, I hosted the workshop, and it went ... surprisingly well.

In fact, I ended up meeting some really cool people, a few of whom decided to sign up to work with me. I really didn't see that coming. But what was even more noteworthy was the shift that I began to notice internally.

That little voice that I had obeyed pretty much my whole life was ... wrong. *Consistently wrong.*

How could this be? Nothing bad had happened. In fact, things kept getting better and better. I hadn't died. I wasn't publicly humiliated. I wasn't rejected by my friends and family. My life wasn't doomed beyond repair. In fact, things were going quite well.

However, if I hadn't publicly committed myself, I can't say for sure I would have followed through on any of these ideas. That little voice seems anything but little when you get close to the edge, it becomes loud and all consuming, but that's the point.

> *There is a level of safety in the known. If we keep doing what we've always done, we can predict the future and that feels safe. But that also feels mundane and stale, and most importantly – it's an illusion. We can't predict the future. No matter how often we avoid taking risks we still don't know what the future holds.*

Besides that, it's human to want growth, to want progress, to want more. And that's what creates such inner turmoil. It's the constant push-pull of that little voice of fear and your innate desire for growth and change.

When we follow that desire for growth, it will inevitably lead us to the edge of our reality, because *growth* in any sense of the word can only happen when we do something new. To fulfill that desire, we have to go against deeply conditioned beliefs that in some way will tell us *it's not possible*. That message may show up as fear and doubt like my experience, or it may show up as procrastination, self-sabotage, or a feeling of inner resistance.

This was the case for Eliza. Eliza had a real go-getter, fiery personality. When we worked together, she was boldly chasing her dreams and building a business that made her feel alive. She was starting from scratch, fueled by a divine sense of purpose and building a business from the ground up with her kids in tow.

Eliza contacted me because she was facing an inner resistance that was inhibiting further growth. It was causing her to feel like she couldn't go all in on her business. She didn't understand where this resistance was coming from and, despite her trying to push through, this destructive pattern prevailed.

In our session I guided Eliza into a trance state and prompted her subconscious to call upon the part of her that caused the resistance. She began to sense a towering, immobilizing door. This part of her was very adamant that the door serves the purpose of keeping people away and blocking forward movement. As we dug a little deeper, the motivation behind this part of her revealed itself. Its purpose was to keep Eliza safe.

This part of her feared that by allowing her business to progress, she would bear more responsibility than she could handle. Between parenting a preschooler, keeping up with household responsibilities, and building this business, she already felt like she was spinning too many plates. Underneath the passion and excitement she felt extremely overwhelmed and unsupported. Raising kids and building a business isn't an easy task, both required a lot of her time. She feared if she allowed the business to get any bigger, it would all come crashing down.

When I suggested asking for help, she felt that getting support felt like giving up control, which only fueled the fear even more. With this new understanding of where the resistance stemmed from, Eliza was able to reframe her perspective of support, which alleviated the fear of asking for help. She realized that getting support actually *increased* her capacity to grow and open up space. By outsourcing to a professional she could focus on growing and scaling her business. Support was the very thing that could make her feel safe. This change in perspective was enough to satisfy the part of her that felt unsafe and resolve the inner conflict causing resistance.

Eliza accepted this new understanding on an emotional level, meaning she didn't just understand intellectually – she actually *felt different*. By reframing her perspective on a subconscious level, we were able to release the emotion trapped in this inner conflict. With the fear released and a new understanding of herself, she watched the door fall down, creating a bridge to support her in reaching her biggest goals and dreams. She no longer felt blocked, and the part of her that held resistance was happy to progress because it no longer felt unsafe to do so.

After the session, Eliza mentioned that she was certainly aware of the stress of parenting and running the business but didn't realize that this was what was causing the resistance in her business. In the days following our session she reached out to a bookkeeping firm to outsource one of her many responsibilities and felt a massive relief. Until the fear was released, outsourcing any part of her business felt impossible and scary. Now, it was the very thing that could support her biggest dreams.

Working with your different parts can be a very powerful tool in resolving inner conflict and negative patterns. It can shed light on the underlying motives that drive your behavior and help bring you to a resolution. Sometimes the inner conflict is obvious, such as my experience of fear and my desire for growth. But other times, the inner conflict that causes sabotaging patterns isn't so obvious. This was the case for Mackenzie.

Mackenzie is a very unique and special woman whom I had the pleasure of working with. She had moved to Thailand a few years back and was working on a business start-up of her own. She was seizing life, and it was incredible to witness.

Mackenzie contacted me because she was struggling with getting out of bed in the morning. It wasn't just as straightforward as sleeping through her alarm; mornings in general would cause Mackenzie to feel a deep sense of dread, which is what kept her in this self-sabotaging pattern of sleeping in. This difficult pattern had been running for years and, no matter what she tried, sooner or later she would eventually revert back to that old pattern of sleeping in.

This pattern was affecting her mornings, but more importantly her mood and motivation throughout the day. Each morning when her alarm would sound, she would feel that uncomfortable feeling of dread wash over her. In an attempt to avoid that dreadful feeling she would consciously or unconsciously choose to roll over and go back to sleep instead of getting out of bed. Not only did she feel like a failure every morning when she didn't get up with her alarm, but that feeling of dread would linger.

In our session, I guided Mackenzie into a hypnotic state and prompted her subconscious to call upon the part of her that had difficulty getting out of bed. She began to sense her younger self and a flood of emotions from her childhood came pouring in. She felt sad for her child self because her homelife was often unpredictable with strangers coming and going at all hours of the day and night. As we dove deeper into that feeling, she was brought back to an early childhood memory of sitting at the top of the stairs, peeking down through the railing at the unfamiliar people in her house. In that moment, she was filled with dread, craving safety and stability.

From this experience, she interpreted life to be unstable and unpredictable. Taking risks of any kind would trigger that underlying sense of dread because deep down she never felt stable and safe within herself. Getting up in the morning actually meant taking steps toward building her business – which inherently meant taking risks. That stored feeling of uncertainty made her unconsciously crave stability and safety, causing her to sabotage her efforts by sleeping in.

I guided Mackenzie to bring her adult self into the memory to be with her child self. She imagined sitting with her younger self at the top of the stairs, comforting her with deep compassion. Just imagining her adult self with her younger self released so much of that fear and dread. The heaviness started to shift. She began to feel safe and comfortable and soon that feeling of dread had completely faded away.

Mackenzie was able to completely reframe this memory and, in doing so, released the heaviness of uncertainty and dread. By experiencing this memory with her adult self there, she was able to understand that the conclusions she had come to as a child were not objective truths. Those experiences did not actually affect the potential she had to create the life and business that she desired.

Guiding my clients to imagine their adult self being with them in painful or difficult memories is a game changer. When we are in a hypnotic state, we are connected with our subconscious mind without interference. That means we have an opportunity to shift long-held beliefs and release stored emotion from prior experiences. By guiding Mackenzie to bring her adult self into that stressful time we could release that feeling of dread that consumed her. She immediately shifted her perception of that experience by seeing it through her adult perspective.

> *In sessions like this we are very careful not to change the memory, but rather change the meaning you assigned to neutral information from the memory. We can't go back and change what happened, but we can reframe the experience and what it meant to you.*

Bringing Mackenzie's adult self into that childhood memory gave her the opportunity to feel safe in an unpredictable environment and reframe the beliefs she had formed. It allowed her to see that she already had everything she needed in that moment. This emotional understanding is what shifts the subconscious beliefs and conditioning. Mackenzie felt empowered and relieved. The feeling of dread in that childhood memory had vanished and she felt lighter.

We wrapped up the session by bringing her back to the moments of her alarm going off and she felt all those good feelings coming with her. She said she imagined her child self in the room with her, jumping around with excitement about the cool place she lived in, and the beach just outside her window. It made her laugh and smile that her inner child would be so thrilled if she could see what a beautiful life she had created.

Moving forward in life and progressing in her business used to trigger that feeling of uncertainty and dread. After this powerful reframe she understood that she was able to take calculated risks and ultimately move forward in life. Sleeping in was an unconscious effort to stop her from doing something she deemed unsafe.

When I checked in with Mackenzie two weeks later she reported that the feeling of dread in the mornings was completely gone. In fact, for the first time ever, she was waking up *before her alarm*, getting out of bed before her boyfriend, and feeling refreshed and ready to start the day. She even noticed a huge uptick in productivity and motivation in her business because that dark cloud of dread no longer plagued her.

We had revealed the unprocessed emotion that had been stored deep in her subconscious. By getting directly to the source of this negative pattern we were able to release the root cause on a subconscious level. Sleeping through her alarm was her way of avoiding risks and uncertainty. This powerful reframe had released the dread and uncertainty that she held in her subconscious. The pattern of sleeping in no longer served a purpose and faded away effortlessly.

> *When we follow that innate desire for growth and begin to approach the edge of our reality, we unknowingly trigger our built-in security system and alarm bells start going off. It's trying to send us right back to where we were, because it believes that place was safe.*

Maybe it shows up as that little voice inside that causes an influx of fear and doubt such as my experience. Or perhaps it tries to slow you down with procrastination and resistance such as Eliza's experience. Or maybe it's an unconscious pattern, like Mackenzie faced, making it feel impossible to move forward.

Regardless of how it shows up it's just your subconscious beliefs creating that Illusion of Limitation. It's not because we're self-destructive by nature – quite the opposite. It's because we have a primal instinct to keep ourselves safe, and *familiar is safe.*

> *When you approach the edge of your reality and begin to experience that Illusion of Limitation showing up as fear, doubt, self-sabotage, or resistance, keep going. By crossing the threshold of that illusion, you are stretching your reality.*

The Illusion of Limitation showed up when I dreamed of traveling across the world. It made me feel like it was unsafe and unrealistic and gave me a million reasons not to do it. And, to be fair, it had some pretty good points: the fourteen hours on an airplane with two kids; the language barrier; being completely on our own halfway across the world, etc. But that deep desire kept pushing me to the edge of my perceived limits, begging me to cross them.

I booked the flights and two months later we were in Italy along with our two kids. I cracked open that Illusion of Limitation and exposed the lies. Then we did it again the following year. And again.

> *The moment you feel the fear and do it anyway, your world expands, and it never contracts. Once you take that step, your reality becomes bigger. Once you do that thing that once felt unrealistic, it becomes real for you.*

The moment we boarded that plane with our kids, it became possible for us to see the world. The moment I signed on my first client it became possible for me to build this business. The moment I spoke in front of strangers, it became possible for me to share my message.

These experiences have expanded me; never again will they feel impossible. They will now always feel possible because I've crossed the threshold and expanded my reality to include them.

So when you notice that Illusion of Limitation trying to stop you, just smile; you are approaching the edge of what you once thought to be impossible. You're about to crack the Illusion of Limitation and cross the threshold into an entirely new reality.

"Each one of us has a three-year-old child within us, and we often spend most of our time yelling at that kid in ourselves. Then we wonder why our lives don't work."

LOUISE HAY

CHAPTER 6:

Accepting the Rejected

I used to think healing was the hardest thing we do. Then I had a baby.

I, like most women who grow a tiny human inside of them, gained weight during my pregnancy. The excitement of seeing my belly get bigger each week was challenged by the anxiety of stepping on the scale. The number grew bigger and bigger each week, as did my thighs, my arms, my face ... you get the idea.

But that wasn't the worst part.

Everybody told me my body wouldn't be the same after pregnancy. On the outside I smiled and accepted their advice, but internally I was rolling my eyes and thinking *watch me*. I was determined that I would get my pre-baby body back. I was sure of it. No amount of weight gain would stop me from fitting back into my old jeans.

But for some reason the idea that my body would change in ways I couldn't "fix" had not crossed my mind. Maybe that's why finding that first stretch mark in the last few weeks of pregnancy was so hard. It was only about a half inch long, but to me it represented my worst fear.

I tried to reassure myself that this wasn't a big deal. After all, one stretch mark wasn't so bad. Then another week passed. Maybe those other stretch marks were already there; maybe they had been there for weeks already, or maybe they all showed up at once, it really doesn't matter. When I saw them in the mirror, I *gasped*.

It felt like shock waves echoed through my body. I was stunned. I knew that this was not something I could fix. This was permanent damage to my body. *Permanent*.

I cried, hard.

And I cried each time I saw them for the next three weeks as my belly continued to get bigger and bigger. The last week or so of my pregnancy was rough. Knowing that each day my belly would grow bigger, stretching my already maxed-out skin even further, and there was absolutely nothing I could do about it.

I gave birth to my beautiful baby girl at 40 weeks 6 days. I was overjoyed to become a mother, and grateful that my baby was happy and healthy. Being heavier than I'd ever been was tough, but I felt certain I'd lose the weight. I was determined to not let anything stop me. However, catching a glimpse of those stretch marks in the mirror would make my heart sink and put a knot in my stomach.

I *hated* my body.

It didn't look like my body, and it didn't feel like my body. I felt trapped in this skin suit that wasn't mine. The weight came off slowly and steadily and was gone in about eight months. I was back in my old jeans, at my old weight, just like I said I would be. But it was bittersweet. They were right; my body wasn't the same, and it never would be.

Maybe healing isn't the most difficult thing we do; I'd witnessed my body healing from the C-section incision, week after week it felt better and better. Healing was the most natural thing my body could do – it's what it's designed to do.

> *Maybe the most difficult thing we do is accept the parts of us that we can't heal. To accept the parts of us that we see as bad, ugly, embarrassing, and shameful. There are parts of us – physically or psychologically – that are difficult for us to look at or accept.*

Unlike my C-section incision, my feelings toward my stretch marks didn't get better each week. In fact, I continued to feel worse; I continued to hate my body. Unlike healing, there was nothing I could do about these permanent changes.

Becoming a mother has taught me so much, it's been the hardest and most incredible experience of my life – cliché, I know. But one of the first lessons it taught me was with those stretchmarks.

There was nothing I could do about the changes my body went through to bring life into this world and hating my body was an unjust punishment. It took a while, but eventually I started to see those scars differently. I started to realize that they were a mirror to the parts of me that I felt embarrassed and ashamed of. I couldn't heal the stretch marks, I couldn't change them or make them go away, and I'm not meant to.

I'll be honest, it's not like I go around parading my stretch marks. In fact, I love high-waisted pants that keep those scars concealed. However, I no longer feel shame and disgust when I see them; they were actually the catalyst for some deeper changes within me. Those stretch marks had revealed to me just how hard I'd been on myself my whole life. My need to constantly hold myself to unreasonable standards was rooted in shame. The need to control everything about my life, including how my body looked was rooted in fear. Perhaps shame and fear had been running the show more than I realized.

Of course, my whole life didn't change the instant I made that realization, but it may have been the first time I felt genuine acceptance of myself. Those permanent scars may have been just what I needed to begin to unravel the layers of fear and shame that were running my life. Those scars taught me how to accept the parts of me that I saw as unacceptable. They taught me to love the parts of me I saw as unlovable. They had shown me that the Illusion of Duality that was causing me to hate fundamental parts of myself was *wrong*. My stretch marks were not bad or something that I should feel ashamed of – they are a part of me; an undeniable part of me.

Perhaps the hardest thing we do is accept the things we see as unacceptable and love the things we see as unlovable. It requires us abandoning everything we used to believe and changing our model of the world.

Those scars were one small step down the path of accepting all parts of me, but that one small step proved that it could be done. It proved to me that I could love the parts of myself that I believed were so unlovable. I could change my perception of myself.

> *"It's a step that most people want to skip (hello!). Most of us want to skim over the part about accepting our most unlovable parts because it's not glamorous. Perhaps there are others like me*

> *who would rather obsess about ways to change the parts of us that make us so uncomfortable rather than doing the work to love and accept them.* 99

Perhaps there are others like me who would do anything to hide and deny the parts of them that cause them to feel shame and embarrassment. I get it. But that's not the answer. The only way to truly move forward is to break free from the Illusion of Duality and see all parts of you with love.

In my sessions with clients, I guide them to see the parts of themselves that they have deeply rejected through a new perspective. I hold space for them to do the work of accepting the parts of them they have deemed shameful or unlovable.

In an altered state this process usually happens without much resistance. Without the chatter of our conscious mind, we can see our rejected parts much more clearly. We can experience a deeper emotional understanding of acceptance. We can more easily shift our perspective and allow love in.

This is exactly what happened with Ava, a very bright and bubbly mother of two. She and her husband were in the process of purchasing a rental home when she contacted me. The process of purchasing the real estate – going through endless paperwork and navigating legal terms triggered a feeling of insecurity and self-doubt within her. It made her feel inadequate and small.

She was a very smart woman, but was entering into a minefield of new terms, concepts and jargon that was all brand new to her. It brought up a feeling that made her think she wasn't smart enough to figure this all out. Unfortunately, she was very familiar with this feeling. Sometimes just having a conversation with someone about a topic she didn't feel fully knowledgeable in would trigger this deeper feeling of inadequacy.

In our session I guided Ava into a trance state and got her to reconnect with that insecure, inadequate feeling. I prompted her subconscious mind to bring us back to earlier times in her life where this feeling was present. One by one, Ava's subconscious presented her with memories where that feeling of inadequacy was present, until we got all the way back to her grade one classroom.

She was brought back to age seven when she was sitting in the classroom with her teacher and parents. The adults were discussing how she was doing in school and expressing their concerns. As that seven-year-old girl, she sat there listening to their discussion and felt incredibly small and inadequate for not learning at the same rate as the other kids in her class.

Ava realized that her perception of herself had shifted in that moment and, from then on, she questioned herself and doubted her abilities. She never really felt good enough, because she carried a subconscious belief that she wasn't as smart as everyone else. She felt judged by others because deep down, she was judging herself. She was rejecting the part of her that she felt was unacceptable.

In the session I guided Ava to see this experience through her adult perspective, and she immediately felt different. She could see that there was no reason for her to feel ashamed. In fact, she could see that her parents weren't trying to make her feel bad at all. They had always been her biggest supporters and continued to be long after this experience. She knew that as that child, she had tried really hard in school, and it was okay that she learned things at a different rate than her classmates. She held so much compassion for her younger self and imagined giving her child self this new perspective.

That inadequate feeling faded away effortlessly. In that moment all she felt was love for that little girl, and without any resistance she accepted this part of her that she's been so ashamed of. With this emotional acceptance she released those old beliefs of inadequacy and could see so clearly that she was just as smart as all the other kids. Even more so, she could see that if she put her mind to it, she could do hard things; nothing was too difficult for her to figure out.

By seeing herself as a child who didn't understand, instead of a child who wasn't smart enough to figure it out, she realized she'd been wrongly judging herself her whole life. That lingering self-doubt that had always lived within her, surfacing anytime she was faced with something new, suddenly evaporated. She shifted a deep identity-based belief about herself and accepted a part of her that she had seen as so unacceptable.

About a week after that session, I caught up with Ava. She told me that she no longer felt intimidated by the paperwork and process of purchasing the rental home. Instead, she dug out the paperwork and began to read through it because she knew that she was smart enough to understand if she gave herself the opportunity to learn.

The level of confidence she felt in herself had shifted because she was able to accept and bring love to the parts of her that she had once felt so ashamed of.

It's life-changing to feel true acceptance, especially when we've been deeply rejecting parts of us for a lifetime.

> **❝** *That self-rejection causes us to believe we aren't really worthy of the things we want in life; be it safety, success or unconditional love. Self-rejection causes a disconnection between what we desire and what we allow ourselves to have.* **❞**

When we feel parts of us are unlovable, we unknowingly sabotage opportunities to feel loved and happy. Realizing that we've been rejecting and denying fundamental parts of who we are gives us the opportunity to see these patterns clearly. This was the case for Jillian.

Jillian is an absolute beam of sunshine. One of the sweetest and most genuine people I've ever had the pleasure of meeting. She was struggling in relationships. She had been married in the past to someone who had been unfaithful, which ended the marriage, and now she was in a new relationship with hopes that he was the one. The problem was she felt like she had walls up that didn't allow her to let anyone in.

In our session I guided Jillian into a trance state where she could connect more deeply with that walled-up feeling. I then prompted her subconscious to take us all the way back to the first time she felt those walls go up and she found herself in a vivid memory of being just two years old.

Her mother had given her a time-out for something she'd done. In that moment, that little two-year-old Jillian felt completely alone and misunderstood. She felt guilty for being who she was. She recalled feeling like she was always in trouble, like she was *too much*. That two-year-old didn't understand that the time-out was the consequence of her behavior but she interpreted the punishment as a consequence of being unloved by the person who was supposed to love her most. She felt like being her fullest self had led to this painful rejection. In those moments she began to reject the parts of her that she believed caused her this pain. Unconsciously she had created a belief that would follow her all throughout life; *being myself isn't safe*.

This belief would show up in her romantic relationships because they were a mirror to that early rejection in love. Any form of rejection, no matter how big or small would trigger those unprocessed emotions that were stored deep in her subconscious and cause her to feel immense shame. Not only that, but because of those deeply rooted beliefs, she would settle for men who would reinforce that shame by being emotionally unavailable or unfaithful. Each time she would allow her most vulnerable self to be seen, they would reject her in some way or another, further validating that deep unconscious belief that being herself wasn't safe. From just two years old she would deny and reject the truest parts of herself because she believed they would always lead to pain.

I'll never forget the conversation we had a few weeks after her session. She realized that early in life she perceived love as something that was unsafe – like getting into a vehicle with someone who would crash the car. Right when she would take down her walls and allow her most vulnerable self to be seen, her partner would metaphorically drive off the road and crash. She felt powerless, like sitting in the back seat while the person she trusted the most drove off the road – again and again.

This was how it felt early in life with her mother, then again with her ex-husband, and the pattern continued. She felt like she would get in their vehicle, and just when she felt safe enough to show the parts of her that felt the most vulnerable, they would crash the car and hurt her again. Over and over, she would feel completely unsafe and rejected by those she loved most.

But she kept getting in the vehicle. Or she would get in with someone else who would do the same thing because deep down she thought this was just what love felt like. She told me that she understands this pattern now and can see it clearly. She understands that love is not supposed to feel this way and the belief that it's not safe to be herself is untrue; instead that was simply the meaning she had assigned to neutral information from her mother. She put walls up because she had believed that parts of here were unlovable. She didn't feel safe in relationships because she never felt safe to be herself. Rejection from her partners further validated that deeply rooted belief that parts of here were unlovable.

She told me she realized that she doesn't have to get into metaphorical vehicles with people who will not drive safely. In fact, she could drive her own damn car as she didn't need to rely on someone else for love and acceptance. She could raise her standards because she truly believed she was worthy of love.

> *Accepting the parts of ourselves we've been rejecting is not an easy task. It requires us to love our most shameful parts unconditionally. It requires us to see ourselves through an entirely new perspective.*

My experience accepting my new body after pregnancy was just the first step on the road to accepting the most rejected parts of myself. It prepared me to love and accept that twelve-year-old me that I'd been so ashamed of. It prepared me to accept the parts of my sexuality that I'd been rejecting.

Life has a way of revealing the parts of us that need healing. When I notice deep feelings of shame, unworthiness, or insecurity, it serves as a reminder to love my most wounded parts. There are no "good" or "bad" parts of me.

There is just me. There are parts of me that I accept and parts of me that I'm still working on accepting.

I'm often reminded of that twelve-year-old girl who I used to see with such shame and embarrassment. I now see her with love. I admire her ability to be herself without the fear of judgment. I continue to strive for her level of self-acceptance, where I no longer see qualities of myself through the Illusion of Duality.

Perhaps healing our darkest parts requires tremendous courage, but accepting our most unacceptable parts requires true, unconditional love.

"Trauma is a fact of life. It does not, however, have to be a life sentence."

PETER A. LEVINE

CHAPTER 7:

Bringing Light to the Darkest Parts

I never planned to heal from my past.

I truly thought I could avoid it forever. It's not that I didn't want to grow and evolve myself, *I loved doing that*. I loved analyzing my patterns and seeing things from new perspectives. I was knee-deep in gratitude and was all about being in the "good vibes". Self-development had become quite a hobby of mine. I'd read new self-help books, kept a journal on what I wanted to create, saw the good in everything, and embodied the person I wanted to become. It was light and breezy.

Healing, however, felt scary and confronting. It required me to face the deepest, darkest parts of me and work through things I'd long buried and suppressed. I never wanted to deal with the deepest wounds I carried; that felt too scary and painful.

The plan was to become "stronger than my trauma"; forcefully suppress those heavy feelings, focus on staying positive, and avoid ever dealing with my past. The problem was that those unprocessed emotions were triggering me a lot. Random, normal things would trigger intrusive memories causing fear or shame. It would literally keep me up at night.

However, I hoped that if I kept trying, eventually I would figure out how to successfully "self-develop" my way through it without ever really dealing with my trauma.

Needless to say, the plan was failing. It still felt like everywhere I went, I was being reminded of the thing I was trying so hard to forget. But what choice did I have? Facing it meant acknowledging it, and I was sure I would never do that. Until, that is, I was sitting across from the woman at the Theta Healing class, and she just knew. In that moment it felt like my worst nightmare coming to life.

> *Little did I know, I was already living the nightmare. It began when I experienced the trauma and because I never healed, it had never ended. Facing the deepest, darkest parts of me was the only thing that would ever set me free.*

I sat in front of her, tears in my eyes, panic on my face as she described what she saw in my body scan – a black spot right at my ovaries. I was terrified because I knew exactly what that was. It was the sexual trauma that I'd been trying so hard to suppress. When she opened her eyes and saw the fear on my face and the tears in my eyes, she immediately knew. She quietly took me to another room where we could talk in private, away from the others in the class. After a few minutes she asked me to close my eyes and began to guide me into an altered state. Through a simple process I was confronted with the weight I'd been carrying. I came face to face with that trauma, but in a way that felt supportive and safe. She guided me to release the fear and panic that I had stored in my body. What surprised me the most was that it felt easy, like a part of me had been waiting years for permission to finally let this go.

She then invited me to forgive myself. Honestly, I didn't even know I needed to. I didn't realize that part of the weight of my trauma was my unwillingness to forgive myself. In that moment, I finally did; I forgave myself for what I had been through and for the weight of carrying it all those years. In that forgiveness, it felt like I could finally put it down. I felt a physical release. It was like there was a tension in my body that was there for so long that it felt normal. And when I let it go ... I felt weightless.

I'll never forget that day because it was the last day of that nightmare. It was the last day of living under the dark heavy cloud of my past. Suddenly it felt like the sun came out and I was being showered with light. It was such a relief. Every part of me felt free.

When I left the class and came home, it felt like I was coming home as a different person. Somehow, life seemed easier; as if I'd crawled out from under something dark and heavy and finally took a deep, full breath in.

I never saw myself as a dimly lit person until I finally put down the weight I was carrying and realized how much brighter I could be. I expected the feeling to fade within a few days, but it didn't. Weeks went by, then months; this feeling was here to stay.

> *Most exciting of all, when I brought healing to that part of me that was hurting the most, it really felt like I had put the past where it belonged – in the past. I was no longer triggered by everyday things. Memories no longer barged in at random times. I wasn't plagued with that same heaviness. It finally felt like something I had been through, instead of something I was still going through.*

When I later learned about healing trauma through Hypnotherapy, it all made sense. The emotion that was stored in my mind and body from that trauma was haunting me. The fear, panic, and shame that I felt was still in there, and it was creating the Illusion of Unsafety. That illusion was affecting the way I saw myself and the way I experienced the world around me. I never felt free from my past because those unprocessed emotions were constantly being triggered. When I faced that wound and released the fear, I could *actually move on* from my past instead of running from it.

We often don't realize that our past has such a hold on us. We don't see all the ways that our painful experiences are still affecting us. I see this a lot with my clients. They contact me with an issue that has surfaced in their life. As we work on resolving the issue, they realize it's actually part of something much deeper. This was the case for Addison.

Addison is an incredible woman and a gentle soul. She has deep compassion for those suffering and has created a life around helping them. Her presence is both warm and powerful, and yet there were people close to her that made her feel small and unworthy. Addison had worked so hard to build her confidence but for some reason those people could pull it all out from under her. She felt powerless and judged in their presence.

In our session I guided Addison into a trance state to connect with her subconscious mind. I then guided her to call upon the part of her that felt judged and unworthy. She immediately saw her child self, feeling scared and ashamed. She told me that, as that little girl, she didn't believe she would ever amount to anything; she never felt good enough. I guided this part of her to follow that unworthy feeling, and it took her back to where it all started.

She went back to a traumatic childhood experience where she felt scared and unsafe in the presence of someone she trusted. I invited her adult self to come in and be the protection she never had in that moment. Addison imagined rescuing her child self from that experience and giving that little girl the protection that she needed. This caused a powerful shift for Addison.

Early childhood trauma can cause us to believe that the world is an unsafe place. When children are in need of safety and it's not available, they may form a belief that safety is never available, creating the Illusion of Unsafety. When that need isn't met early in life, the unsafe feeling becomes their model of the world. It affects the way they see themselves and the way they interpret situations, even into adulthood. In contrast, children who receive safety and protection early on learn that they are safe. It's not that they learn to become dependent on somebody to save them, but rather, they learn that they have the ability to save themselves.

> *Offering ourselves protection in our darkest moments may be the most powerful thing we can do. As a child, protecting ourselves often doesn't feel like an option. Children are easily manipulated into believing they can't go for help, or there's no way out. To release that intense fear and unsafety, I invite their adult self to be the protection they needed.*

As soon as Addison imagined protecting her child self in that experience, she felt a massive sense of relief. It was over. The fear and panic were immediately released. It's as if her autonomic nervous system understood that the threat was over, and it could ease back into a restful state.

This is the kind of shift that creates lasting change. Not only have we released the fear and panic, but we've also created an emotional understanding that she can trust herself. She is her own safety. We haven't changed the memory; Addison still remembers what happened to her, all we've done is release the fear from that experience and shattered the Illusion of Unsafety that had continued to make her feel unsafe and afraid.

I checked in with Addison a few days later and she reported feeling lighter. She said it was like something had been released, it felt like she took her power back. She also mentioned how powerful it was to protect her younger self in that experience. She felt more connected to her inner child than ever before and said that she imagined having her child self with her at times, doing things that her younger self would have liked – she even stopped in for an ice-cream cone, something she hadn't done in years but felt like her child self would have loved.

When we release the underlying emotion that's been trapped in traumatic experiences it shatters the Illusion of Unsafety and creates a shift in how we see ourselves and the world around us. Things that used to feel scary or intimidating no longer have that effect on us. For Addison, the Illusion of Unsafety caused her to feel fear in circumstances that were non-threatening, such as being authentically herself around those people. Releasing that unresolved fear from her past had freed her of those heavy feelings and given her a new sense of confidence.

That unprocessed emotion isn't always fear; it can also show up as anger, too. This was the case for Samantha.

Samantha was extremely hard working and diligent in her pursuit of life. Even in her early twenties, she already understood many of the hardships of life from her lived experiences, which only made her a more compassionate and caring individual. She was the kind of person who would do anything for the people she cared about.

Samantha contacted me to work on her anger. She felt that her everyday interactions triggered a level of anger that wasn't warranted. Normal things like a family member asking about her day when she got home would cause her to lash out.

She didn't know where this anger was coming from; it felt random and unexpected. In our session I guided Samantha into a trance state and got her to connect with that angry feeling. I guided her subconscious mind to regress back on that feeling and show her where the unprocessed emotion was being stored.

She found herself in a painful childhood memory where she had suffered the loss of someone close to her. She was nine years old when a friend died suddenly and unexpectedly. This experience caused her so much pain. She felt a deep sadness for the loss of his life, but also such anger that he was taken from her. This loss, especially at her age, was hard for her to understand. She didn't know how to cope with someone so young passing away; it felt cruel and unfair.

This experience had been so painful that she was unable to process the emotion she felt. The anger and sadness had been trapped in that experience and was affecting her now, nearly a decade and a half later. We took our time working through this loss. We brought her adult perspective in to help her younger self understand. Because his life was taken so suddenly, she never felt like she had closure. In our session we could alleviate some of that pain by imagining him there with her. She was able to say the things she never had the chance to say and finally feel some closure for his death.

Grief is a complex emotion, and we wouldn't expect to move through it in a single session. It's a process of acceptance that happens over time. In our session we were able to relieve much of the anger of losing him and help bring some understanding to this painful experience. It was as if she was coaching herself through the loss, comforting her younger self and shifting her perspective of his death.

By the end of the session Samantha still felt a level of sadness, as we would expect from losing someone we love, but the intense anger that she felt had greatly decreased.

I checked in with Samantha a week later and she reported her anger had dramatically subsided. She didn't feel like she had to try to control the anger anymore, it simply didn't show up like it used to. She felt relief. That anger that had been stored from that experience was heavy, and finally processing that emotion was like a weight being lifted.

> *Healing the deepest, darkest parts of us may be the scariest thing we do because it means facing our most painful wounds. Self-development often feels light and breezy compared to the work of actually healing those wounds. Healing feels confronting and scary but, in the end, it's the only way to truly move forward.*

If I'd known I'd be facing my deepest trauma at that Theta Healing weekend I would never have gone. But if I'd known how much better I'd feel after bringing light to my darkest parts, I would have never waited so long to do it.

Bringing healing to our most painful experiences is life-changing. Protecting ourselves in the moments where we felt the most vulnerable creates a sense of strength and safety within. Even the darkest parts of us don't seem so bad when we let the light in.

"The body doesn't know the difference between an experience and a thought, you can literally change your biology, chemistry, hormones and genes, simply by having an inner event."

JOE DISPENZA

CHAPTER 8:

Solving the Chronic Equation

Our body is the vessel that we use to experience life. Nothing is more detrimental or enhancing to our existence than the health of our physical body. Yet for most of us, when it comes to healing our body, we feel completely clueless. When pain strikes or disease manifests, we immediately hand all of our power away and accept our fate. Why? Because we are living in an illusion that tells us that without a medical degree, we are incapable of healing ourselves. This illusion tells us that without understanding the complexities of our bodily systems we are unable to heal. This illusion causes lifelong suffering and a sense of helplessness in our quest for health.

The Illusion of Separateness will have us believe that what's happening in our body is completely separate from what's happening in the mind. However, this couldn't be further from the truth. We learned this back in Chapter Four.

The mind and body are completely intertwined. They are two parts of the same system, working simultaneously with each other. The body is speaking a language that we instinctively understand right from birth. All throughout our day, our body is sending us signals that enable our survival.

When time has elapsed since our last meal, our body will send us a signal to eat through the sensation of hunger. If we didn't have this hunger signal, we may go too long between meals and eventually suffer malnutrition, or even perish. When we consume something that could be potentially harmful, our body may send us a signal of danger through the sensation of itchiness or nausea. If we've expended our energy and need to replenish our body through sleep, our body will send us a signal to rest through the sensation of fatigue.

Our body has these built-in signals to ensure our survival and our continued existence in this body. Without any of these sensations, we may find ourselves in very dangerous or harmful situations simply because we may not be aware that something is wrong.

The body has various signals that alert us to possible danger or problems. We are born understanding that those signals mean that something is wrong; they are a signal of distress. When the distress signals continue for months, years and even decades, we categorize these signals as chronic conditions.

Science has gone to great lengths to understand chronic pain, illness and disease on a micro level, and yet chronic conditions continue to become more and more prevalent in our society. According to the Public Health Agency of Canada, 44% of Canadians aged 20 years and older have at least one of ten common chronic conditions. In the United States, that number is even higher, with over half the population struggling with at least one chronic condition. We understand chronic pain and disease on a cellular level better than we ever have, and yet chronic conditions are more prevalent than ever before. Perhaps we have become very good at finding the answers to all the wrong questions.

> *Perhaps the Illusion of Separateness has us believing that the solution to the body's dis-ease can only be found under a microscope or in a prescription bottle. The Illusion of Separateness will have us believe that the mind has no influence on the body and, therefore, has no part to play in the creation of disease or in the healing.*

This illusion will cause us to believe that chronic pain, illness, and disease are unexplainable phenomena happening at random. It will cause a further disconnection from the body because we then see our body as weak and frail and see healing as complex and out of our hands.

Breaking free from this illusion lies in the fact that we need to understand that the mind and body are deeply intertwined, and that the distress in the body is often a mirror for the distress in the mind. When distress signals such as pain, fatigue, nausea, or itchiness remain for months or even years, it is paramount to ask the right questions.

> *The body does not randomly fail. Systems do not randomly break down. Pain is never a random coincidence and disease is never an unexplainable phenomenon. Newton's Third Law of Motion states that for every action, there is an equal and opposite reaction. Pain, illness, and disease are the result of some prior force; they are the equal and opposite reaction.*

When dealing with chronic conditions, this *prior force*, or in other words "root cause" is the answer to healing. To permanently heal your body, you need to resolve the *cause* of the pain or disease.

As discussed earlier, pain and disease are distress signals from the body. To heal, we need to relieve the distress causing the dis-ease. However, this distress may not be so obvious; it may be *unconscious stress* that has been stored in the subconscious mind. This means that the stress has been repressed for so long that the conscious mind no longer remembers. But that doesn't mean it goes away. That simply means it's been buried. The conscious mind has suppressed the stress, but the subconscious mind continues to experience it.

I refer to this stress as *unconscious stress* because it affects our thoughts, beliefs, actions, bodily functions, and perception of reality without our conscious awareness. It's causing havoc on the inside without us even realizing it. As we learned in earlier chapters, that unconscious stress is unprocessed emotions from big "T" or little "t" traumas from our past. Experiences where we felt a high level of distress without the ability to process our emotions can result in stored stress in our subconscious mind.

That stress may become triggered in everyday life by non-threatening experiences, resulting in danger signals from the body such as unwarranted anxiety, shame, anger, or pain.

> *When our subconscious mind is in a hypervigilant state where it perceives danger around every corner, it may react by perceiving certain sensations or aspects within our body as dangerous. This causes our body to interpret safe sensations as painful, fight our own cells, or fight cells that are not dangerous, resulting in a variety of conditions from chronic pain and inflammation, to allergies, and even autoimmune disease.*

On the outside, it appears that pain and disease come out of nowhere with no cause, but under the surface, the body has been perceiving all information as dangerous. The unconscious stress in the mind causes a level of stress in the body that may go undetected for years.

Then perhaps some kind of distressing event happens, such as divorce, loss of a loved one, or unemployment and suddenly the body cannot handle the stress any longer, resulting in a chronic diagnosis.

Or perhaps nothing distressing happened prior to the chronic diagnosis. Perhaps the buildup of unconscious stress had slowly reached its breaking point where the stress on the body begins to show up as pain or dysfunction in the body. Similar to the onset of a flu; you may have encountered the flu-causing virus yet have no flu symptoms for several days. Although you encountered the virus, it had to multiply millions of times over the course of several days before you begin to feel sensations of illness. Is it correct to say that the sensation of a sore throat is the beginning of the illness? Or is it correct to say that the illness was present much before you detected the first symptom?

> *Just like the onset of a flu, the diagnosis of chronic conditions is not necessarily the beginning of the condition. Your body has likely been in distress for years or even decades before you detected the first clue that something was wrong.*

I describe the cysts that appeared on my ovaries during a stressful period. Perhaps that singular stressful experience was enough to cause dysfunction in my ovaries, or perhaps my body had been living in constant unconscious stress for years prior, since the sexual abuse occurred.

Likewise, I describe the bursitis in my hips as showing up several weeks after a very distressing experience with the loss of my childhood dog. Perhaps the distress from that experience was enough to cause inflammation in my hips, or perhaps my body had been carrying unconscious stress prior to that experience. Regardless, one thing is clear: the distress in my body was mirroring the distress in my mind.

Our healing requires us to become detectives, solving the chronic equation.

Chronic Pain and Disease = Chronic Distress

Listening to our body's distress signal and following its clues will lead us to the cause of the distress. In Hypnotherapy sessions I guide my clients into an altered state where they have uninterrupted access to their subconscious mind. I then prompt their subconscious to call upon the part of them connected to the pain or disease. Often, the subconscious mind will reveal varying levels of traumatic experiences and unprocessed emotion that's been stored on a subconscious level. These distressing emotions are what's causing distress in the body, and ultimately leading to physical pain and disease.

As we learned in Chapter Four, trauma can dysregulate the autonomic nervous system, increasing the risk of chronic disease later in life. This is because it activates the stress response in the body for prolonged periods of time. Our body is meant to go in and out of a stress response but is not made to live in a constant state of stress. It's as if our body is continually preparing to fight off a threat that no longer exists. It may be years or decades after a distressing incident and the body continues to feel threatened as if the threat is still ongoing.

Any experience, no matter how big or small that causes high levels of distress could be enough to send the nervous system into the sympathetic response.

Furthermore, when the trauma happens in childhood it can have lasting effects on the developing nervous system, causing it to stay in a hypervigilant state.

Getting to the root of physical pain and disease can illuminate the stress that our body has been holding onto, even if our conscious mind no longer remembers.

Meet Callie. Callie is a delightful young woman with big dreams and a warm personality. She contacted me to help her work on the pain and symptoms of her polycystic ovary syndrome (PCOS), which she had been suffering with for several years. In our session, I guided Callie into an altered state where I prompted her subconscious to call upon the part of her connected to the PCOS. Immediately, Callie began to sense a pink worm shrinking and sinking down into itself. She got the sense that this part of her felt ashamed, the shrinking was an attempt to become small and hide.

I guided Callie to tap into the feeling of shame and prompted her subconscious to regress to the cause of that feeling. She was taken all the way back to a memory of being just three years old, when she'd done something to make her mom upset. The shame she felt for upsetting her mom was overwhelming. Even at just three years old, she felt guilty for doing something wrong and not feeling able to make it right. In that moment, all she wanted to do was shrink down and hide. Her body had carried that unprocessed shame and guilt all throughout her life.

I invited Callie to see this experience through her adult perspective and right away she could see that she had nothing to be ashamed of. Instead, she saw a little girl who was doing the best she could. With that understanding, she could finally release the shame she had carried all those years. The part of her connected to the PCOS was the part of her carrying the shame. The heavy burden of shame had lasting effects on her nervous system and was wreaking havoc on her body and causing symptoms of PCOS.

Callie felt a massive weight being lifted in that session. I caught up with her a week later and she reported her menstrual cycle changed suddenly on the day following that session. One symptom of PCOS is an unpredictable menstrual cycle. After five years of irregular cycles and unpredictable menstruation due to her PCOS, she eventually went on to have two normal 28-day cycles following that session. This was completely unheard of for Callie.

We had resolved the unconscious chronic distress which was the *cause* of her pain and symptoms. It had been a buildup of shame that weighed heavily on her for nearly her whole life. Callie had no conscious recollection of that memory, but her subconscious stored it all. When she released that underlying shame, she noticed an immediate positive effect in her body.

Getting to the root of chronic pain and disease is sometimes an experimental process as we follow the distress cues in the unconscious mind. When this unconscious distress is released, it can have life-changing effects. This was certainly the case for Charlotte.

Charlotte was a nurse practitioner diagnosed with Fibromyalgia, Chronic Fatigue Syndrome, chronic migraines, and cluster headaches. At the time that we met, Charlotte had quit her job because the pain and symptoms were so severe it made working unbearable.

She lived in constant pain, ranging from skin and muscle irritation to nerve pain and migraines. Some days it was more intense and debilitating, other days it was more of a dull hum in the background, but it was always there.

When we met for our initial consultation, Charlotte seemed eager to dive into her subconscious and was willing to do whatever it took to see changes. She said something in that initial meeting that stuck out with me: "Even if my symptoms improve just 10%, it would be worth it."

That might not seem significant, but to me that told me everything I needed to know. Charlotte wasn't there for a miracle cure or a magic pill to eliminate her pain. She wasn't there because she needed me (or anyone else) to "fix" her. She was there because she wanted to improve her quality of life. As a nurse, she was already doing everything possible to manage her pain and symptoms and was open to trying anything that would cause her to feel better in her body.

This mindset is crucial to the success of the sessions. It tells me that she is open to seeing results but isn't expecting a miracle to happen overnight. I've found that clients who are desperate to see changes will be more likely to give up hope if the results aren't immediate. If they've decided for any reason that the process won't work for them, further sessions are futile. I needed her to be on board with me. I needed her full participation and belief that it's possible to see changes.

In my mind, any change, no matter how significant or slight, shows us that progress is possible and that the process is working. But if the expectation is to have immediate results and "cure" your body, the slight shifts in symptoms or pain will go unacknowledged and faith in the process will evaporate.

Those who have accepted where they are, are much more resilient to the ups and downs of healing and have more patience for the process to unfold. They notice the slight changes, and they see that as worthy of celebration.

In our first two sessions, Charlotte's resilient mindset held strong as little by little we gained clues to the emotional connection of her chronic conditions. On our third Hypnotherapy session, I guided Charlotte into a trance state and prompted her subconscious mind to follow those emotional clues. She was immediately shown memories where intense emotion had been stored. Her subconscious brought us back to a childhood memory where she felt unsafe. During that session we were able to release that unprocessed emotion and restore a feeling of safety within her. The next day I received a message from Charlotte.

She woke up with *no pain*. She was shocked.

Less pain was normal, dull pain was normal, but *no pain*? That was unheard of for Charlotte. I was excited to hear about her progress, knowing that this meant we were on the right track, but kept in mind there may still be more to work through. The next day I woke up to another message. *Still no pain.*

Then again the next day ... and the day after that. Two weeks went by until our next session and still the pain she had lived with for the last several years was gone. She was thrilled to report that the pain and symptoms of the Fibromyalgia and Chronic Fatigue Syndrome were seemingly gone, however, the chronic migraines were still showing up.

Our fourth Hypnotherapy session was focused on getting to the root cause of the migraines. Using a similar technique, I guided her subconscious to reveal the stored emotion connected to the headaches and again Charlotte felt a massive shift as she healed the deep wounds from her past.

Weeks went by with no pain or symptoms. The migraines had vanished. Not only did Charlotte resolve the stored emotion in her subconscious, but she also gained an understanding of herself and the connection to her pain.

The pain and symptoms were no longer the enemy – they were the messenger. Her body had simply been a mirror for the emotional pain she was carrying.

Over the weeks that we worked together, she began to understand the message that her body was communicating and went on to make big changes in her life. She realized that the life she was leading was contributing to her stress. She decided to make big moves in her career, going after something much more fulfilling. Her physical and emotional health is now her highest priority, and she regularly makes decisions that support her overall wellness.

It's been over two years since Charlotte and I worked together and she continues to be pain free. Even her seasonal Cluster Headaches that regularly occurred every second spring have ceased to exist. Charlotte gave up much of the things in her life that were contributing to her stress and is now completely in tune with her physical and emotional wellbeing.

The Illusion of Separateness between your mind and body will cause disconnection and leave you feeling helpless and vulnerable. Coming to the understanding that our minds and bodies are completely entangled can be life-altering.

> *Healing the root cause of pain and symptoms can reveal emotions buried so deep we no longer remember feeling them; but that doesn't mean they disappear. They still exist, buried beneath our conscious awareness, causing havoc on the inside. When we can access the deeper awareness of our subconscious, we can solve the chronic equation and start to heal.*

Resolving the underlying root cause is one of the most important steps in healing. Often the answer to our suffering is overlooked because we are searching in all the wrong places.

We are receiving communication all the time from our mind and body in the form of pain, dis ease, destructive patterns, and emotional upset. But if we're not listening, the messages will go unheard, and the suffering will continue. Our job is not to "fix" ourselves with the latest medical trend, but rather to stop and actually listen to what our body is telling us.

PART 3
THE
GROWTH

"She understood that the hardest times in life to go through were when you were transitioning from one version of yourself to another."

SARAH ADDISON ALLEN

CHAPTER 9:

Shedding the Skin

I believe we live two lives.

I'm not talking about reincarnation or alternate dimensions. I'm referring to *this life* and the way we choose to live it. As Confucius, the great Chinese philosopher, once said, "We have two lives; the second begins when we realize we only have one." That was certainly the case for me.

There's a period of my life that feels hazy. Not because I can't remember it, but more so because it all kind of looked the same. The years blend together in my memory because I was living on autopilot.

By society's standards I was progressing in life. I graduated high school, fell in love, held down a few jobs, saved money, bought a house, got married, etc.

But as far as where I wanted to go, it felt like I had hardly made any progress at all. To be fair, it's because I wasn't doing *anything* to move my life in that direction. It's almost like a part of me just thought one day things would magically be different and everything would just fall into place. It's almost embarrassing to admit that

I didn't realize that if I wanted something completely different, I would have to *do something completely different*. My tiny, suffocating little reality made a lot of things feel out of reach. My life was never the same after that lightbulb moment on that misty August morning back in 2015.

> *I didn't go from lost to found in an instant, but it cracked open my world and made me believe that I could be more. It made me feel like anything was possible. It caused me to think about what I really wanted out of life, and it gave me the courage to begin my second life.*

Prior to that life-changing day, I had never had the courage to follow the things that lit me up. Following that lightbulb moment, I began to do things I'd been too afraid to do before. Writing was something I'd always loved, but for a long time, I'd denied it out of fear that I would be judged and ridiculed. However I was feeling more courageous than I ever had, so I bought my first domain and started a blog, Sun Kissed Kate.

Buying the domain for my blog symbolized the beginning of my new life. A life where I made decisions based on what I wanted to create in the world and the impact I wanted my life to have. I had no idea what I was doing, and it didn't matter. The idea that I had a little slice of the internet to create whatever I wanted was so exciting.

In the beginning I didn't tell anyone about my blog. It was my little passion project and was the very first step outside my comfort zone, so I was being very cautious. I had the courage to create the blog and share my writing, but I sure as hell wasn't brave enough to tell anyone about it.

Writing and creating posts for my blog was fun and exciting. It was so fulfilling to do something just for me. This was the first time ever that I had the courage to do what my heart was calling me to do. I worked on my blog daily, for months. I would get up early and stay up late. I would write blog posts when my daughter napped and spend all my spare time researching Pinterest strategies and SEO – *I felt so alive!*

After a few months of writing, I started to focus my blog posts on living a clean, non-toxic lifestyle. I was researching ingredients, experimenting with my own recipes, and reviewing my favorite non-toxic products. My sister and I would get together and get busy creating all kinds of DIY projects – from lip balm and hand lotion to laundry soap and bug repellent. Then I would snap photos of our creations for the blog. I even created social media accounts and had clean beauty brands sending me free products in return for a feature. It was a wild ride, and I was completely consumed.

All the while I felt like I was living a double life. Most people just saw me as the new mom, bringing her daughter to play groups, grocery shopping and going for walks. But behind closed doors, I felt like I was creating a life that I had only ever dreamed of.

Out of fear of being found out by my peers, I kept my full name off the blog. Instead, I went by "Kate".

> *Over time, 'Kate' became my alter ego – the version of me that was courageous, confident, and successful – everything I felt like I wasn't. Katie was busy changing diapers and scrubbing Mac 'n Cheese off the highchair with her new baby, but Kate was fearlessly pursuing*

> *her dreams. Without consciously deciding to change, I began to embody Kate.* **"**

My style began to change and become more sophisticated like I imagined Kate would be. I even started experimenting with makeup; lipstick and shimmery eyeshadows were now in rotation. I picked up new hobbies like yoga and meditation. I became more disciplined with my time, waking up early before my daughter and spending naptime working toward my vision. I became more of a *doer*, instead of just a dreamer.

In the grand scheme of things those steps seem pretty small. Going to a yoga class, writing blog posts and wearing lipstick once in a while doesn't change your life. However, those little changes symbolized the bigger changes happening inside. I started to realize that I could be someone I had never been before. I could be the person I imagined myself being. *I could be Kate.*

Having the confidence to change my style and pick up new hobbies created a momentum that grew bigger and bigger. Pretty soon, I realized Kate was the kind of person who has *been places* and *done things*. She was the kind of person who's seen the world.

It was Kate who insisted on booking that first trip to Europe. Something I'd always dreamed of doing but Katie would never have the guts to do.

Kate just got more and more exciting as I continued to embody her. What I loved most about Kate was that she was entrepreneurial. She was here to do big things. *What big things?* I didn't know; I hadn't got that far yet. But Kate was definitely the kind of person who didn't let anything hold her back. Kate was the kind of person who knew what she wanted and went for it. The more I embodied Kate, the more alive I felt.

Kate's life was interesting and exciting. She was worlds apart from who Katie was. After eleven months of blogging in secret, filling my cabinet with free products and growing my blog to nearly 50,000 unique visitors per month, I finally told my friends and family.

All this time I had been working so hard. I had been at my computer every single day. I had been committed to a goal and nothing stopped me, not even the fatigue and nausea of my second pregnancy. I was doing something that, in my mind, was *really big*.

And I was *really* proud of myself.

I felt like a snake, quietly creating a whole new me under the surface until I reached the point where the old skin had to start coming off and start to reveal the new me.

My biggest fear was what others would think of this new me. That fear kept that whole project a secret for nearly a year. I felt extremely vulnerable, like I was showing a part of me that I hadn't let anybody see before.

Most people I told didn't understand my excitement because they'd never heard of a blog before. Others reacted very nonchalant, telling me that they had also thought about starting a blog – making me feel like the dedication I'd put into this project was insignificant; *anyone could do it*. Some acted like I'd just told them it might rain next week; hardly news worth asking questions about let alone celebrating.

It was a hard hit, but it was Kate that kept me going when I felt most vulnerable. *Katie* may have folded under that pressure. *Katie* may have wanted to hide when people saw who she really was. But

Kate was fearless. Kate would never let someone else's opinion of her change her course. Kate got brighter when someone tried to dim her.

I buckled down and within the next year I doubled my blog traffic. I had never been more dedicated to being successful at something, and it felt so good. I felt powerful. Most people still made me feel like it was just some silly hobby, but to me it was proof that I could create an entirely new world for myself – proof that I could be successful. Kate was the fire inside that decided she wanted something and didn't stop until she made it happen.

This momentum that I'd created by embodying Kate is what led me to pull the trigger on signing up for that very first Life Coach training program in 2018. It was a $5000 commitment that Katie would probably have talked herself out of – Kate said. *"Fuck, yes."*

By that time, I was three years into embodying Kate. My life felt so different because I saw myself so differently.

> *Without realizing it I had shed my old skin, the parts of me that were weighing me down and keeping me small. Sure, I wasn't totally fearless. And yes, I definitely still had work to do on myself, but I'd shifted who I believed I was, and that's what made everything else possible.*

Katie would never have signed up for the Theta Healing course that caused her to face her deepest trauma and begin to heal. Katie would never in a million years choose to speak in public or candidly share her story.

It was the embodiment of this new self that made all of this possible. It was the beginning of my second life when I finally came alive. Although my life changed dramatically as I embodied this new me, after a while I realized Kate had to go.

I remember the day that Kate died. I was finishing up the Life Coach training and preparing to officially launch my new Life Coaching business into the world. This required a brand new website which required a brand new domain. But what would I name it? What name would symbolize the passion and devotion I had for this new venture?

The answer was obvious: my name; my real name. *Katie*.

Kate had to go; or rather, the separation between Kate and Katie had to go. Kate was no longer my alter ego, she was me. I had fully integrated every part of her into who I was. And best of all, I didn't feel like I had to hide behind a name anymore, *Katie* was confident and fearless. *Katie* was determined and focused. *Katie* was doing the work every single day to build this new life. Stepping into this new chapter would mean owning this person that I'd been growing into over the last three years. It was time to fully shed the old skin and embody who I'd become.

Shortly after integrating Kate and embarking on this new adventure, I knew it was time to let go of the blog. Running the blog and trying to build my business felt like trying to run in two different directions at the same time. In a way, it felt like the blog had become a distraction to what I ultimately wanted. Although I cherished that small slice of the internet, the lessons it taught me, and the success that I'd achieved, I knew that it served a purpose on my journey, but it wasn't meant to be forever. Letting my domain expire and my blog be erased from the internet forever was hard. But sometimes hard decisions are necessary.

This was the first of many hard decisions I would have to make as I pursued this new life. Little by little I would need to let go of many things that I clung to in my old life that were keeping me small. Little by little I would need to step further into the unknown where nothing is guaranteed, and nobody is going to catch me when I fall. But that's what made my second life so different.

That August morning was the catalyst that began my new life.

> *At first nothing changed except how I saw myself and the world around me. But slowly I began to morph, like a snake growing a new skin beneath the surface – the changes had to happen on the inside first. Then when I'd grown to reach the limits of that old me, I could start to shed that layer and emerge as an entirely new self into an entirely new life.*

Shedding can be uncomfortable for snakes and can make them feel anxious, not unlike shedding old parts of ourselves. To be able to grow into a more expanded version of you, you have to let go of the old. And it's completely normal to grieve that old life and that old you. I found myself at many times along this journey grieving the old me and the life I'd once lived because it had become so comfortable and familiar. This new life was intimidating and required a lot of courage.

To create the vision I had for my life I needed to continually push myself into new environments and new challenges. It meant being vulnerable as I learned and experimented, and feeling extremely humbled when things didn't go as planned. Since then, I've continued to grow new versions of myself and shed old layers. I still feel vulnerable each time my new self is presented to the world, but it gets easier each time because I realize it's a necessary part of living this second life.

Transformation doesn't happen in an instant. It's a gradual process of slowly shedding the stale, stagnant and heavy and becoming anew. It's a vulnerable process that requires courage and stamina. With each new evolution you become more alive than you ever thought possible.

With each old layer shed, you come closer to that raw expression of self that you were born to be. Your second life starts the moment you decide to start living it.

"The two most important days in your life are the day you are born and the day you find out why."

MARK TWAIN

CHAPTER 10:

Beyond the Self

I sometimes wonder if the experience of an existential crisis is unique to the human experience. And if it is, is it because we have evolved past the basic needs of survival? Do we feel this intense urge for meaning and purpose because we no longer spend our days outrunning prey and searching for our next meal? Do we feel conflicted by the concept of the meaning of life because our basic needs – food, water and shelter – are readily available?

I can't say for sure, but I do know one thing with certainty. There is a question that has plagued me, day and night for nearly my entire life: *Why am I here?*

This question has always lingered in my mind, but in times of stress, struggle, or conflict it seemed irrelevant. Perhaps those challenges caused me to feel like my basic needs of survival were being threatened. Suddenly it's like, *Who gives a shit why I'm here? I just need to get through this.* Then, just like clockwork, those challenging times would end, and that haunting question would return.

I believe that our journey of self-development, growth and healing will ultimately lead to this question. As we begin to make sense of ourselves and heal our wounds, it's natural to want to make sense of our world and heal others too. As we crack open that little reality and reach for more, our focus shifts from the self to the collective and we feel an urge to contribute to something greater than ourselves.

I felt this urge right from a young age, before life's challenges distracted me, and I've felt it in every moment in between. As far back as I can remember I had this feeling like I was here for a reason. Not like a twinkle-in-my-eye kind of feeling, but more like an urgent pit-in-my-stomach kind of feeling. I felt like me being here was no coincidence, but rather, that there was some urgent matter I needed to attend to and time was ticking to figure it out.

But I wasn't one of those people who knew from a young age what I would do with my life. My siblings seemed to have a better idea than I did, and when they graduated high school, they each went on to college to pursue those plans.

I just kept stumbling; battered with that nagging feeling like I had an important job to do and time was running out. It's like I had this very unique puzzle piece that I needed to place. I kept finding different jobs and hobbies to see if it would fit, but nothing did. I looked around my small town at everything that was available to me and felt even more discouraged because nothing made sense. I would go from job to job hoping that within those four walls I would find what my soul was urging me to do. I was desperate.

Before I had my first child, I had started University courses to study Real Estate Appraisal, thinking that maybe this would satisfy the feeling. I worked at a private appraisal firm, then moved onto our local Provincial Assessment office in hopes that I'd finally found my purpose.

However, after just a few courses I went on maternity leave and came to a massive realization that none of this was right. In the pursuit of meaning, I felt like I lost all meaning. In trying desperately to *find* my purpose, I felt like I got further and further away from it. I couldn't find anything that seemed to fit, so I started forcing it.

> *Just like forcing a puzzle piece into the wrong spot, it didn't feel quite right. Deep down I could sense that something was off, even if it looked good on paper. But just like a puzzle, that incorrect piece becomes more troublesome when you try to connect the next piece and it doesn't fit right either. Then the next. Pretty soon the whole puzzle looks pretty fucked up, and it all comes back to that piece you tried to force that just wasn't right.*

A lot of people ask me how they can find their purpose. Turns out that "here for a reason and time's running out" feeling was not unique to me. Lots of people feel this way.

And I tell everyone the same thing: *"Stop searching.* Your purpose is not 'out there', it's 'in here'."

What I learned from my own experience was that I may never have "found" my purpose by searching for it because even if I stumbled across it in my desperate attempts, it wouldn't feel like the right one because I hadn't embarked on the *journey of finding it.*

Back then, I didn't even know who the heck I was, so how could I identify my purpose in this world? I hadn't even gone through the most pivotal moments in my life that would cause me to feel so passionately about the work I do today.

Never in a million years would I have guessed that I would become a Hypnotherapist. Never in a million years would I have guessed that my purpose and passion would be facilitating sessions and holding space for people while they dug up and processed the most wounded pieces of them. Never in a million years did I see myself as someone with the capacity to fulfill this purpose.

So even if I would have stumbled across this job in my many internet searches, I really don't think it would have lit me up like it does today.

> *I really believe that there were important steps that I had to take 'in here' before anything 'out there' would have made sense. I believe that I had to find myself before I could understand what I'm here to do. And trust me, I was a stranger to myself back then.*

This reminds me of one of my favorite sessions. I was working with Sophie, who reminded me of myself and the journey that I've been on. She was desperately searching for her purpose and had contacted me to help her figure it out.

In our session I guided Sophie into a trance state, then prompted her subconscious to sense the part of her that was seeking meaning and purpose. She was immediately shown a beautiful orange and black butterfly. At first, the butterfly was frustrated and felt stagnant. It was just sitting still, feeling unsure and nervous about where it should go and where it would end up. I felt called to point out that the big, beautiful wings of the butterfly offered her infinite options. I noticed the expression change on Sophie's face when she realized this. It wasn't long before the butterfly was ready to fly and finally took off.

She described the movement of the butterfly as seemingly erratic and unpredictable, but that's just how it appeared from the outside. Inside, the butterfly was simply following inspiration, going wherever she felt called to go without judging the decisions.

She realized that when she released the need to know where she would end up, it gave her the freedom to feel inspired. The pressure to go in the right direction faded away and she allowed herself to just land on the flower that felt right in the moment. Sophie told me that there were no wrong stops when she was the butterfly because each flower would lead her to the next. The metaphor of the butterfly has stuck with me because I believe it perfectly symbolizes the journey of finding our purpose.

> *In the beginning we don't know where we will end up – and we're not supposed to. We're just supposed to start flying, and land on anything that lights us up. And when we feel called to move on, the next step will become clear. We can't be given the answer because the journey is an essential part.*

Looking back at my own journey, it is clear to me that my life had meaning the moment I decided to do what lit me up. That first decision was creating my blog. My blog led me to writing about ways to improve our lives – starting with non-toxic products then leading into mindset shifts. This excitement led to my life-changing weekend at the Theta Healing course where I faced my deepest trauma, which inspired me to guide others through deep transformation. The desire to go deeper into the most vulnerable parts of the human experience eventually led me to Hypnotherapy, energy work and Pain Reprocessing Therapy where I now work with individuals to help them heal from anxiety, trauma, and chronic pain.

Today, I feel certain of my purpose, and feel called to share it with as many people as I can, which is why I'm here, writing this book. If someone would have told me ten years ago that I would work with people on pain, anxiety, and trauma I would have laughed. *Not a chance!* But the journey that led me here has prepared me for what I believe is my life's purpose. I'm sure it will continue to evolve just as it has all along.

There are no cheat sheets when it comes to finding purpose and meaning, but as I progressed along my journey, I found a few tools that I've used to help understand myself and what I'm here to do. These tools shouldn't replace what you know to be true about yourself but, in my experience, they can help navigate the unfolding of your most authentic self.

Astrology was the first one I came across. Years prior I had looked up my zodiac sign and was *thoroughly unimpressed*. Clearly it was way off because I couldn't relate to any of it. Back in those years when I was drifting through life, not really sure of anything – including who I even was – the things I would read about myself according to astrology made no sense to me.

But as I slowly started to untangle myself from who I thought I should be and started to become who I truly was, astrology made more and more sense. It's not that I was trying to align my life to what the astrology said I would be like. In fact, it wasn't really until I was on my current path that I realized everything that didn't make sense before made perfect sense now. Astrology isn't the answer to that looming question, but I've learned that it can be a tool when we are beginning to figure out who we are in this world.

Not all of it will resonate, of course. But on my journey, it really helped me solidify who I thought I was. At that time, it felt like a boost of confidence. Over the years I've used astrology as a sounding board to what I feel about myself. I think that relying too heavily on astrology (or anything for that matter) can certainly be a detriment, but if it confirms to you who you feel like you are on a deeper level, then it can't hurt.

Astrology is an abundance of information, which can quickly become overwhelming. If you are new to astrology, I would recommend starting with the big three: your sun, moon, and rising sign, and once you feel ready, moving onto the other layers of your chart.

Your sun sign represents your ego and motivations; your moon sign represents your emotional nature; and your rising sign speaks to the energy that you put out into the world.

Your sun sign can be easily found by correlating your date of birth with the twelve zodiac signs that loosely follow the months of the year. This is really the most basic part of your chart and where most people end their search. However, if you can find out the exact time and location of your birth, your chart will begin to make much more sense.

When I was able to get my exact time of birth, I could pull up my birth chart with full accuracy and it confirmed to me so much about my personality, motivation, and what makes me feel so alive in life.

As an example, I was born mid-November, so I am a Scorpio sun. Scorpio suns are known for feeling at home in the darker sides of life and are always ready to investigate. The nitty gritty details intrigue them, and they possess the strong passion to heal, create and transform.

My moon is in Virgo, which reveals that my emotional nature is of the analytical, practical type. This placement thrives when life feels organized, structured and practical. Following routines that ultimately create order in my life is of high importance.

And finally, my rising sign is in Capricorn. Capricorn placements are known for being ambitious self-starters who are mature and responsible. This placement has great staying power and has the ability to focus on long-term goals that don't have immediate gratification.

When I learned this about my chart, it made so much sense to me. My Scorpio sun placement explains the passion I feel for my career as a Hypnotherapist, working on the deepest, darkest parts of the human experience and helping individuals process heavy emotions and pain. I've always had an entrepreneurial spirit, and the Capricorn placement confirms that dedication and sense of responsibility I've always felt. Finally, my Virgo moon will make sense to those that know me personally. I am a sucker for routine, and I am happiest when I can analyze and organize all parts of my life.

Reading this now makes so much sense to the direction I've taken in my life and why it feels so right for me. But ten years ago, this was complete nonsense! None of it aligned with me because I was so out of alignment with who I was. It wouldn't make sense until I had unraveled all the parts of me that weren't authentic.

As I continued this journey of self-discovery, I eventually came across Human Design and I couldn't wait to sink my teeth in. Your Human Design chart is similar to an astrological birth chart, however, it doesn't just map out where the planets were when you were born, it also identifies your dominant chakras to create your personal body graph.

Your Human Design chart tells you not only *who* you are, but also *how* you are. It describes the best way for you to operate in this world according to your design. A Human Design chart has many pieces that make up the whole; so many that there's too much to list in this section. However, if you look up your chart, a lot of information is available online.

When you enter your birth information you are shown a diagram that resembles a human body consisting of shapes, lines, colors, and numbers. Throughout the diagram there are "centers" connected by lines called "channels" and "gates" (depending on if they're colored in or not).

Some of the aspects of your chart that I will briefly discuss are your *energy type*, which is how you exert and exchange energy with the world around you, as well as your *profile*, which represents how you see yourself and how others see you.

There are five energy types: Manifestor, Generator, Manifesting Generator, Projector, and Reflector. Your energy type will help you understand how to optimize your unique energy in all aspects of life. As an example, Generators "generate" energy constantly – they are like the energizer bunnies of the world, whereas Manifestors are the initiators but don't necessarily have the energy to see things through.

Understanding my energy type validated so much of what I was feeling in my own life. As a Manifesting Generator (MG), I have endless energy for the things I'm passionate about – and MGs are also known for being multi-passionate people.

This is probably why I passionately dove into learning about Life Coaching, then Theta Healing, then Neuro-Linguistic Programming, then EFT, then Hypnotherapy, then Medical Hypnotherapy, then Reiki, then Breathwork, then Pain Reprocessing Therapy ... you get the idea.

Having a business where I can integrate multiple passions is very aligned with my energy type and probably why my career continues to be so fulfilling. This also explains my desire to dig in and spend my energy doing the work. Not everybody feels this way. Projectors and Manifestors likely don't have the consistent energy to sit down day in and day out to do the work, and therefore make better managers and visionaries. Neither way is better, it's all about understanding your energy type so that you can create a life that's most aligned to you.

The other main thing I'll touch on is your Profile. You may find that you can be the same energy type as someone but have more in common with somebody that has the same Profile as you.

Your Profile consists of two numbers, the first number representing your inner archetype and the second representing your outer archetype. Your Profile explains how you see yourself and how others see you.

As a 3/5 Profile, my archetypes are the Martyr and Heretic. This means a lot of what I do in life will be trial and error to find what "works" and what doesn't. I will seek out a variety of stimulating experiences, make a lot of connections, and also leave a lot of it behind in search of what is "right" for me and what isn't. It's a process of discovery and pioneering.

The 3/5 Profile has the ability to initiate a profound transformation within society because once they've found something that really works – whether in their career, relationships, hobbies, etc. they then share their findings with the world.

Again, this makes so much sense for me and the path that I'm on. I feel like something inside of me is in constant search of newness and knowledge. If I were to compare my multi-passionate self to someone who's dedicated themselves to just one thing, I might feel flaky or indecisive. Understanding that this urge for diversity is part of who I am and what makes me unique has led to so much self-acceptance. I can lean into this part of me that wants to experiment and seek newness and know that this is how I'm meant to be.

My goal in sharing these tools of self-discovery is to inspire you to follow what lights you up, because I believe that's what we're here to do. When we get our minds and bodies out of survival mode, and seek something beyond ourselves, that desire for purpose becomes louder. However, we'll never find our purpose if we are living on autopilot. These tools have helped me see parts of myself that I'd overlooked and shown me that what makes me different is also what makes me powerful.

> *Ultimately, the journey we embark on will lead us to a life of purpose. There are tools that can shed a new light on what makes you tick; however, they won't tell you what you're meant to do in this life – that's up to you to decide.*

The courage to flutter your wings and follow your intuition will ultimately lead you to a fulfilling, purposeful life.

> "The wound is the place where the light enters you."
>
> RUMI

CHAPTER 11:

Spiraling Upward

After working on my past trauma I was incredibly relieved. It felt like something I'd been running from was no longer chasing me. I felt liberated and empowered.

Naively, I actually thought I was done healing. As if it was a one-and-done thing. I thought that not only would I never have to touch that trauma again, but there was nothing else I would need to heal either. *Boy, was I wrong.*

You've probably heard the phrase *healing isn't linear,* usually shown beside a line graph with many ups and downs but ultimately moving in an upward direction. I used to see healing this way too; there are ups and downs but ultimately moving toward "healed". But as I worked with more people and journeyed further down my own path of healing, I came across a new way of seeing this healing process.

Healing is a spiral.

We are continually faced with circumstances and experiences that will trigger the wounded parts of us. Before we become conscious of the connection between our subconscious beliefs and our experience, we may just go around in circles in an endless loop. We will continue to face the same painful experiences again and again, maybe with new people or in new places, but always triggering the same wounds.

We cannot exit the loop until we become conscious of our unconscious patterns and take responsibility. When we realize the key to healing exists "in here" and not "out there" we begin the journey inward and that endless loop starts to spiral upwards.

Looking within, it becomes clear that we've been experiencing the world through the many illusions of our beliefs and conditioning. It's a significant moment in life where we begin to see our own experience differently. This realization can be extremely liberating and empowering, but it can also be painful. The loop becomes a spiral when we begin unraveling the illusions and healing our deepest wounds.

As we peel back the layers we begin to spiral upward. With each upward spiral we grow into a more evolved self. However, that spiral will eventually lead us back around to those wounded parts of us. You might continue to be faced with people and circumstances that will trigger that wound, but it's only an opportunity to heal even deeper.

> *You might become irritated and think, I thought I dealt with this already, and you'd be right. You have dealt with this already, and now it's time to face it again as a more evolved self.*

You'll still feel that ping of pain as it triggers that wounded part of you, but this time, you're able to heal a deeper level of that wound because you perceive it from a new perspective. Every journey around the spiral gives us an opportunity to heal another layer of ourselves. We may not always use this opportunity to grow, and instead blame others or take on a victim mentality. All this does is prolong this level of healing. The longer it takes us to take responsibility for our wounds and triggers, the longer we are stuck on that layer of healing.

I had done many loops running from my deepest wound, only to have circumstances and experiences trigger it again and again until I finally faced it. In that moment my loop began to spiral upward. I released a lot of heaviness and a lot of fear, and I felt liberated. But eventually I would loop back around and experience new circumstances that would trigger that wound in a new way. It took me a few loops before I realized that there was more healing for me to do.

I finally understood that the fear and anger weren't the only layer of that wound I needed to heal. This is when I discovered the shame I'd been carrying regarding my sexuality. It was showing up in sneaky ways that I couldn't see at first, but more and more I realized that underlying shame was affecting many parts of my life. So around I went again, going inward and healing that wound on a new level, spiraling up again.

Obviously this isn't the only wound I have to heal. This spiral continues to trigger more wounded parts of me in need of healing. For a long time I felt frustrated, thinking, *I thought I already dealt with this.* Now I realize that I did deal with it, but healing is not a one-and-done process.

> *As long as we have the privilege of breath in our lungs and blood in our veins, we have the opportunity to continue up this spiral. Going inward won't always be a healing session led by a practitioner. It might look like a reflective moment in solitude, or a tough conversation with a loved one.*

Being a parent has illuminated many areas in need of healing and given me some of the most profound opportunities to heal and evolve.

I've had the pleasure of leading hundreds of hours of healing sessions and, from what I've gathered, we make another pass around that spiral and are exposed to the next level of our healing only when we are ready. Unfortunately, it's not possible for us to heal everything at once. We are supposed to unravel the layers one by one and evolve into the self that is prepared to heal the next level.

That means that you and I are not done. We will probably never be done, and that's okay. That's what life is all about. We don't need to obsess about self-development or spend all our time working through our belief systems; we simply take it in stride. When you feel that ping, like something has struck a wound deep inside, you'll know that an opportunity has presented itself. Your triggers are an invitation for growth and healing; going in is the only way to go up.

"It doesn't really matter who you used to be, what matters is who you've become."

ROBERT TEW

CHAPTER 12:

Take Flight

The past several years of working with and studying the subconscious mind has taught me that our entire experience of reality is an illusion. It has proven again and again that our minds assign meaning to neutral information that can cause us lifelong suffering. Every experience that we've been through has contributed to the illusion of who we are, what we deserve, and what we're capable of.

My goal in writing this book is to pull back the curtain and show you that you are wildly capable. You are capable of healing from your most painful wounds. You are capable of shedding the heaviness of your past, and you are capable of healing your body. Reality is completely malleable. The so-called "truths" that we live by have been made up; the unbreakable rules are a fabrication of our imagination. You are capable of incredible change. You can end your suffering.

In Part One we unravel the web of lies that have created our reality. Step by step we dismantle the illusions that we have been living in for a lifetime. Chapter 1 reveals the Illusion of Limitation that causes self-doubt, procrastination, and resistance. Chapter 2 exposes the Illusion of Duality that leads to shame, insecurity, and self-hatred.

Chapter 3 outlines the Illusion of Unsafety that contributes to fear and anxiety. Chapter 4 illuminates the Illusion of Separateness and sheds light on the emotional connection to physical pain.

Part Two is the healing, where we become the person that shatters those self-made illusions. Chapter 5 dismantles the Illusion of Limitation and expands our reality. Chapter 6 is about releasing the Illusion of Duality and coming home to ourselves. Chapter 7 is undoing the Illusion of Unsafety that our trauma has caused us. Chapter 8 cracks open the Illusion of Separation causing healing on a physical level.

This brings us to Part Three, the growth. In Chapter 9 we shed the skin of the person we once were so that we can expand into our next phase. Chapter 10 is the inevitable crisis when we grow from self to beyond the self. And finally, Chapter 11 reveals the next level of healing in your journey.

My wish is that the wisdom in these pages be a gentle reminder of your own courage to rise up, to heal, and to thrive. When things seem hard remember that it takes just a single crack to shatter the illusions and invisible boundaries that have kept you stuck.

You are a beautiful butterfly. The struggle you endure to break free from your cocoon is necessary to strengthen your wings. Everything you've been through has brought you here to this moment. Your pain and suffering have not been in vain. It might seem scary to make the leap, but you were never meant to stay on the ground. You were meant to fly.

ACKNOWLEDGEMENTS

There are many people who have helped bring this book to life, whether they knew it or not. I want to thank every person who has believed in me, right from the beginning. There were so many people who saw my potential before this book materialized, even before I saw it myself.

My parents and my **siblings** who heard me say, "I'm going to write a book one day" ever since I was a kid and they never doubted me.

Jennifer Fritsma was one of the first people who supported me as I journeyed down this new path in life. She saw something special in me, and I'll never forget that.

Cheanise Bidulock and **Mari Roberts** for supplying the spiritual guidance that I needed to get this book out into the world. These two women are incredibly gifted.

Lynnette Fritshaw stoked that fire within me anytime I fell into fear or doubt. The journey of writing this book was insane, and I'm not sure I would have made it through if it weren't for her support.

My sister, **Megan Roux,** was my emotional support throughout this process, but also throughout my whole life. I am so grateful for her.

My husband, **Braydon**, is my rock, my safe place. Trust me, I needed that a lot. **My kids, Nataleigh and Jon,** were my little cheerleaders and biggest motivations for this book. I want you two to know how wildly capable you are, and that no matter what you want with life, it's possible.

Tarryn Reeves helped turn one of my biggest dreams into a reality, and I'm forever grateful that our paths crossed.

I would **also like to acknowledge all of my clients**, including those who gave me permission to share their stories in the book. This book wouldn't have been possible if you hadn't first trusted me on your journey, and I do not take that lightly.

From the bottom of my heart, thank you. It has been an absolute honor to hold space for every one of you.

ABOUT THE AUTHOR

Katie Potratz is a Clinical Hypnotherapist specializing in the areas of anxiety, trauma, and chronic pain. She believes that to live a wildly fulfilling life, we must be courageous enough to heal the root cause of our pain and retrain our brain.

Katie resides in Canada with her husband and two children.

You can connect with Katie at www.katiepotratz.com
Instagram: Instagram.com/katiepotratz/

www.ingramcontent.com/pod-product-compliance
Lightning Source LLC
Chambersburg PA
CBHW040742020526
44107CB00084B/2840